UPHOLSTERY
TIPS AND HINTS

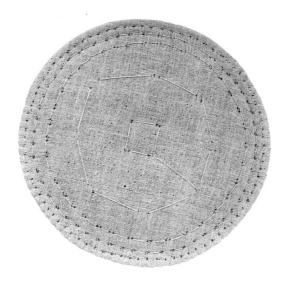

UPHOLSTERY TIPS AND HINTS

David James

Guild of Master Craftsman Publications Ltd

ACKNOWLEDGEMENTS

I would like to thank all those who helped to make this book possible:
Carlota de Aymerich Aspeitia, Angela Burgin, Eileen Crotty, David Edgar,
Eric Fox, Diane and Cliff Gill, Jake Kaner, Campbell Norman-Smith, Inge
Paterson, Len Rentmore, Pavin and Mario Sadat-Dier.

Also the following for their generous support: Rapesco Ltd, Singer UK Ltd,
High Wycombe and District Camera Club, The Guild of Traditional
Upholsterers, The Association of Master Upholsterers and Soft Furnishers,
and the Faculty of Design, Buckinghamshire Chilterns University College.

Finally, a sincere thankyou to my editor, Lindy Dunlop, and to Stephanie
Horner, at GMC Publications.

First published 2000 by
Guild of Master Craftsman Publications Ltd,
166 High Street, Lewes,
East Sussex, BN7 1XU

Copyright in the work © Guild of Master Craftsman Publications Ltd
Text, photographs and illustrations copyright © David James

ISBN 1 86108 168 5

A catalogue record of this book is available from the British Library

Designed by John Hawkins
Cover design by Guild of Master Craftsman Publications Design Studio
Typeface: Monotype Bembo
Colour origination by Viscan Graphics (Singapore)
Printed in Hong Kong by H & Y Printing Ltd

CONTENTS

INTRODUCTION

Are you sitting comfortably? If you are, then it is likely that your seat is well upholstered. Practising upholstery for a number of years inevitably allows you to gain a collection of useful tips and hints, either acquired from experience or passed on by others. Some you like and use a lot, some you may try and then discard. Experience of this kind is a collection of knowledge of the many different ways there are of doing various tasks. It is something that we draw on when needed and when we have a problem to solve. The more methods and tricks we collect, the more rounded and more interesting will be our approach to the work we do. No matter how sure we may feel that we are doing something well, there is always another view or another approach to achieving the same result.

For me, there is always a certain fascination in watching others ply their craft, especially when it is in a skill that I am very familiar with. As you watch, you can appreciate the placement and use of the tools, the manipulation of the materials, and the way in which a technique is often made to look effortless. The tips and hints in this book are set out in alphabetical order for easy reference. They are simply a collection of accumulated ideas.

One of the most common ways of discovering a new technique is taking an old chair apart, removing the original upholstery carefully, layer by layer, to find that it reveals something interesting that you have not come across before. The older the chair, the more fascinating can be the discovery. On page 75 you will find a chaise longue which has a detachable back rest. This was designed and made for easy removal, and can be relocated onto the other side of the seat, so making the piece usable as a left- or right-hand chaise longue. This, for me, was a recent discovery and goes to show that traditional upholstery is never dull. It is an old and fascinating craft, which can be full of surprises.

I hope that these hints and tips will help you to enjoy, as I do, our ancient craft. Are you still sitting comfortably?

David James
January 2000

BACK TACKING

As long as you have a length of stiff card, or some buckram, or a strip of folded webbing, back tacking is a technique you can use very often in upholstery. It is mainly used as a finishing method, for all types of covering. It gives a clean, well fixed line to arms, backs and borders.

There are four stages to good back tacking:

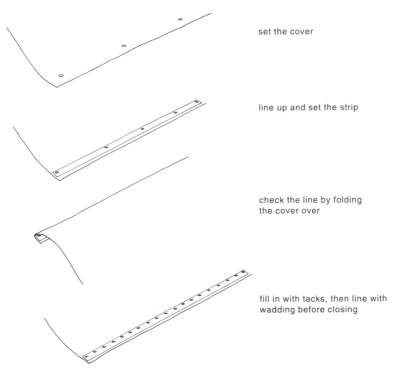

set the cover

line up and set the strip

check the line by folding the cover over

fill in with tacks, then line with wadding before closing

The process of back tacking

1 Set the fabric on with a few spaced tacks and check for straight lines or patterns.
2 Place the tacking strip in line with the finished edge and tack each end taut, then fill in with a few well–spaced tacks along the strip.

3 Bring the cover down, check the line produced by the edge of the strip and that the fabric is aligned and straight.

4 Fill in the spaces with plenty of tacks close to the outer edge, setting about 25mm (1in) centres (ie, 25mm (1in) from the centre of one tack to the centre of the next).

There are many variations of this formula, but this method works for most straight edges on outside backs, outside arms and various types of border. Even some difficult curved edges can be back tacked with care and some thought, though covers may have to be shaped and trimmed to fit before attempting to back tack.

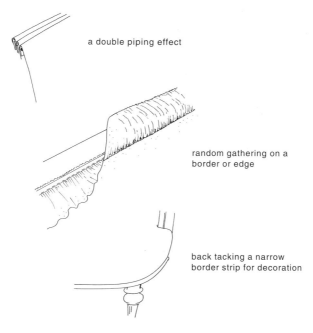

a double piping effect

random gathering on a border or edge

back tacking a narrow border strip for decoration

Examples of back tacking techniques

Using back tacking techniques, different effects can be created; some examples are illustrated here. Back tacking against a trimming such as a piping, cord or ruche always gives a good finish on a chair.

The direct stapling method can be used successfully on suitable fabrics

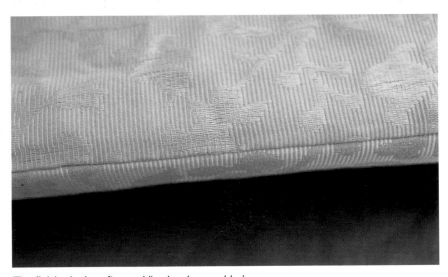

The finished edge after wadding has been added

There is no doubt that the staple gun has many advantages when covers are to be back tacked and finished. Fabrics can be gathered or pleated by direct stapling, with or without a tacking strip. This uses many staples but is fast and easy. A long-nose staple gun is an excellent tool for dealing with difficult areas of back tacking, where a hammer would be impossible to use.

Back tacking the cover and supporting hessian at the same time

For a good finish on the outer covers of chairs in traditional upholstery, back tack the supporting hessian and the cover at the same time. You can then bring down and tension the hessian before adding the wadding and, finally, the cover.

BED HEADBOARD DESIGN

A headboard for a single or double bed need not have an elaborate or sculptured shape. It can be a simple rectangle or a curved shape of MDF, chipboard, or plywood. The appeal of its general design can be created using carefully chosen fabrics and a little creative upholstery. Buttoning, gathering, pleating and bordering are all effects commonly used to produce interesting work. However, a fairly simple, plain treatment, using fabric with texture, pattern and colour, can be equally effective – and much less demanding as a piece of upholstery. The addition of a piped edge or a border to give a smart finish may be all that is needed to create something bright and striking or low key and more restful.

The emphasis for such an approach is in the finding and choosing of a cover or blend of covers to create the desired effect. Having chosen the fabric coverings, or at least obtained some small samples or options, you can juggle with possible treatments.

A small collection of examples is shown to whet your appetite.

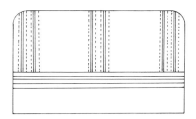

Vertical lines sewn to a striped baseline

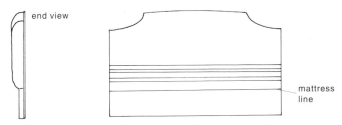

end view

mattress line

The base of the curtain can be used for colour and line

Fabrics can be
cut and joined
to create a
bold design

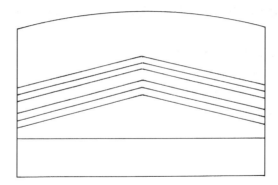

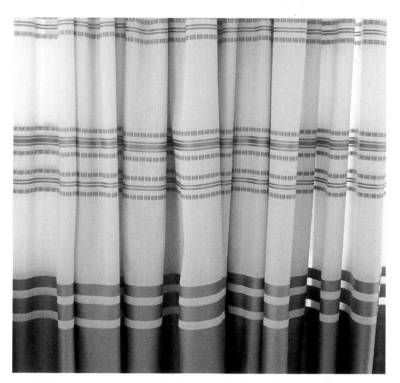

A curtain can be used as a headboard cover or matched in a room treatment

BOLSTERS

From the middle of the eighteenth century the bolster, described as a long supporting pillow, became an integral part of upholstery design. English and French beds, settees and daybeds were designed to have bolster cushions to support the user.

Thomas Chippendale, in his drawings of 1754, shows that at that time, the oval or round pillow was a very important feature, both visually and as a practical necessity. Some years later, the bolster was very evident in Thomas Sheraton's designs and drawings for upholstered furniture and bed furnishings. Some 60 years after that, in the late Regency and early Victorian era, it was still an essential feature of the chaise longue and the sofa.

After a long period of absence, the bolster is in vogue again today, although not dominant as it once was. It is used in various forms, both fixed and loose. The bolster is a friendly and very usable furnishing accessory.

There were several fillings used in bolster making which remained evident until the mid-twentieth century. Curled hair, wool fleece and wool flock, and feathers. All have a different feel and give a different degree of support. These are the fillings that remain in use today, with the addition of loose cotton and, of course, plastic foams and polyester wadding for modern upholstery design.

By far the most common shape for the bolster is the familiar round, cylindrical one. For such a bolster, to be stuffed with any filling other than hair, make up an interior case to the size required, from scrim, ticking, or cambric, then fill and close. The bolster is now ready for covering in upholstery fabric, and for trimming to be added as desired.

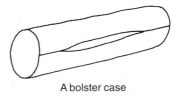

A bolster case

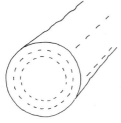

A hair-filled bolster
interior stitched up in scrim

A hair-filled bolster must have a scrim or fine-woven linen case and will need further preparation. After making up and filling the interior case, firm each circular end by mattress stitching, and add tuft or stab stitching along its length to stabilize the filling and hold the round shape.

Bolsters can be, and often were, trimmed and decorated to make them interesting. Pipings, cords, tassels and braids can all be used, along with gathering and pleating of the covering fabric. The choice of decoration will usually be determined by the period or particular style of the furniture being upholstered.

Three parts of a simple bolster cover; the piping strip has been reversed for contrast

The cover made up and filled before the ends are closed

Gathering the ends by hemming and using a draw cord

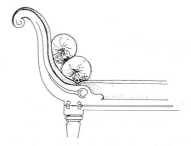

Two bolsters are sometimes better than one

BOXING A CUSHION COVER

An unbordered, box-shaped cushion cover, made to fit a chair or settee seat, for example, is one of the simplest to make up. It requires a ready-made interior of foam and polyester or a feather-and-down-filled case.

To find the required size for the cover, measure for length and width, taking the measurements from exactly halfway down the outer edges of the interior – where the seam line will appear on the finished cover – and add 10mm (⅜in) for sewing all round.

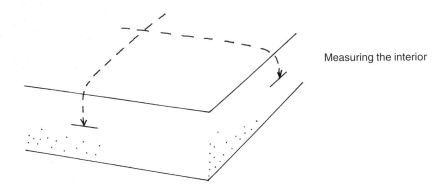

Measuring the interior

Cut two pieces of the covering fabric to this size and place them face to face, ready for sewing. Sew round the outer edge leaving a gap for filling at the back.

The sewing line

Fold, pin and mark the corner

Boxing the corners

To make boxed corners, fold each corner into a triangle shape, with the seams central, and pin in place. Mark a chalk line across each, set at the height of the interior corners less 10mm (⅜in). To finish, sew across each

Tie off the seam thread at each end, and then trim

The boxed or envelope corner

Checking the finished cover

one and trim off the excess to within 10mm (⅜in) of the new seam line. Turn the cover face sides out and check the seams for alignment. The cover is now ready to be filled.

The length and width measurements taken before sewing should be reduced a little if a tighter, more snug fit is required. This is often the case with foam-filled interiors. Making the cover to fit shaped interiors is also possible; again, this will need to be allowed for at the measuring and fabric cutting stage.

Seams for cushion covers with boxed corners are usually kept plain through-out. However, they can easily be top stitched after making up if required.

BUTTONS

There are a number of button sizes available to upholsterers, but the three sizes of round buttons that are most common are 22, 24 and 28. The largest of these is 28, which is about 18mm (¾in) across. These tend to be used mainly for surface buttoning in modern upholstery. By far the most common size for traditional work is the medium size, 24, which is about 13mm (½in) across. This size relates well to traditional chair backs, seats and arms, and is especially suited to deep or diamond buttoning.

I have noticed that the original buttoned upholstery taken from Victorian, and some Edwardian furniture, has a button size a fraction smaller than our size 24. Of course, we can only use the sizes that are available to us and size 24 is our nearest equivalent.

The smallest button of the three is about 10mm (⅜in) in diameter and goes well on any small-buttoned panel. Particularly when the diamond size is about 100 x 65mm (4 x 2½in) or less, size 22 is the best choice. Size 24 looks far too clumsy on small work. It is often small details like this which make the difference between ordinary work and something rather better.

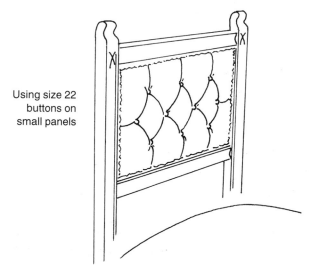

Using size 22
buttons on
small panels

Re-covering buttons

When new buttons are not available, then the old buttons taken from a chair can be re-covered. Try cutting a disc of the new fabric just large enough to go round the back of the button, then glue the edges to its back, without covering the hook or loop. With careful working of the fabric, and some gathering in and snipping with the scissors, a neat, smooth button face can be produced. The finished button will appear a little larger than the original, but will be suitable for deep buttoning where only the face is visible.

Matching button coverings with upholstery

It is important to match the covering on buttons to the areas on an upholstery fabric. When the exact positions of the buttons are known, the

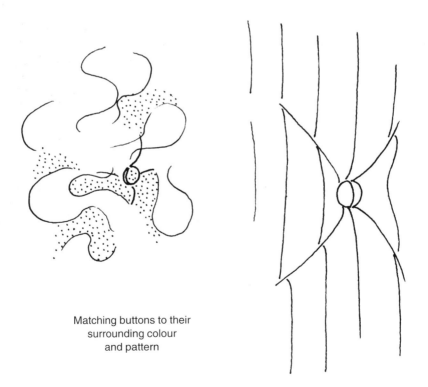

Matching buttons to their
surrounding colour
and pattern

pattern or colouring should be matched from the button disc. This is usually obvious, especially where a cover has plain and patterned areas, and when striped covers are being used. The wrong colour button in the wrong place will draw the eye immediately and spoil a whole panel of work.

Buttons should be matched to the background

CORDS

An upholstery trimming cord can be changed to suit your requirements when an exact colouring or size is not available. Most of the cording used for upholstery has a distinct style compared with those used for costume or soft furnishings. They have three pre-wound or gimped smaller cords or plies twisted together to make one large cord. Cords vary from using only one colour to having a mixture with all three of a different colour, or a two and one mix. Quite often, when a piece for a small job is needed, the exact colouring is not to hand.

two-colour cord

three-colour cord

small cord

Various styles of upholstery cord

A cord with three gimped plies

Taking out one small cord of a dominant colour and replacing it with a length from another can solve the problem. Alternatively, removing one of the cords and not replacing it, but winding the remaining two up tight may also give you what you want. Removing a single cord and rewinding in this way will reduce the size, which can be very acceptable for certain jobs, particularly for surface decoration or on fluting. Playing with cording in this way will also use up odd lengths left over from previous jobs.

Removing a ply to change the colour or reduce the size of the cord

Occasionally, a particular part of a chair or sofa needs a smaller, finer cord than the main cord. Again, this is a good opportunity to vary the size, but do keep the colour of the cording uniform throughout the one piece of furniture. Removing one of the cords from a three-ply cord does need to be done very carefully. All the ends should be sealed with Sellotape before beginning and one end of the cord should be pinned to a bench weight or held to a table edge with a bulldog clip while you remove a ply, so that the whole thing doesn't disintegrate. Equally, one end needs to be held stable if you are replacing a ply.

A flanged cord

Upholstery cords can be made with or without a flange (see page 47). This is a narrow ribbon of fabric, blind stitched or overlocked to the cord by machine. A flange can be removed easily by carefully snipping the stitch line. There are occasions when the flange on a cord is very useful, in particular, when machining it into a joint, but when a length is to be hand stitched in place, the flange is not needed. This is something to bear in mind when you are buying cords. If you see the colour that matches or suits the fabric, then it is of no importance whether it is flanged or not.

COURSES AND SOURCES OF INFORMATION

Books

There are a number of good books on the subject, and whilst a book will not give you the skills required, they are an excellent reference and will widen and confirm your knowledge. A good book will usually answer the age-old question, 'What do I do next?'.

Training

In most colleges of Art, Design or Technology, a course in upholstery of some kind will exist. Depending on the area and the nature of the college programmes, the course may be part time evening, part time day, or full time. Make enquiries at county level about Adult and Continuing Education.

For those who want to try upholstery for the first time, a local Adult Education Centre is a good place to enquire. Joining and working with a group of like-minded people is an excellent way of developing your interest. If you have space for a workshop of your own, this will enable you to progress slowly on your own between class meetings.

There are also many centres throughout the country where weekend and summer school courses are run in arts and crafts subjects. Upholstery is usually listed as a traditional craft.

In craft magazines and periodicals, courses of various kinds are advertised and are becoming very popular. Short residential courses in upholstery are run throughout the year in private workshops. These may be from a few days to a week long, or more, and are a very good introduction to the subject.

The City and Guilds of London has existing and new vocational qualifications in traditional and modern upholstery. City and Guilds will advise as to where these courses can be taken and will provide outline syllabus information. The new Level II qualifications in upholstery commenced in 1999. These are progression awards 6955, and will be available at Level III in 2000. The awards are based on a conventional structure of practical coursework and written examination.

For those who wish to take up upholstery as an occupation, training in a factory or a small workshop business are the two options. Factory work is most likely to be in modern upholstery and will be somewhat repetitive. However, the wages are good and opportunities can be an incentive. The small business in upholstery is likely to be more traditional and give training in a variety of work. The traditional skills of the craft will inevitably take much longer to learn, but will be rewarding and very satisfying in the long term. Good luck!

Trade organizations

The upholstery trade has two registered bodies who represent the craft and who exist to promote good trading. Anyone who wishes to take up the craft seriously can get help and advice about the trade as a whole through these bodies. The Association of Master Upholsterers and Soft Furnishers and the Guild of Traditional Upholsterers both give advice and help to those wishing to embark on training and working in the industry.

The National Training Organisations (NTOs) cover a large percentage of employers in the UK. The furniture industry is represented by a group called the Furniture, Furnishings and Interiors National Training Organisation ˙(FFINTO), who work collectively for the industry on training. The group is led by four major trade and training organizations: The Association of Master Upholsterers and Soft Furnishers, The British Furniture Manufacturers Association, North Lancs Training Group, and WEBBS Training. At the time of writing, FFINTO is working towards accreditation as an NTO with the Department of Education and Employment.

COVERING CONCAVE CURVES

A fabric cannot be forced to stretch over an inside curve when it is concave. The only solution is to snip the fabric at several points along the curve and then ease it over and fix it with temporary tacking. The more the fabric is snipped, the smoother it will become; the number of cuts must be as many as the fabric demands. Each cut produces a short tongue of fabric, which needs a tack to hold it tight. Usually some vertical or lengthways stretching will help to smooth the surface as you progress with tacking.

Curves that require this treatment are very common on upholstered furniture. They include wings, C-scroll arms, the tops of chair backs and some loose seats. In many such cases a facing or border is applied over the cutting. Alternatively, the answer may be a tailored cover.

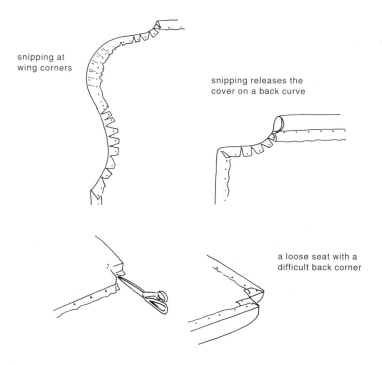

snipping at
wing corners

snipping releases the
cover on a back curve

a loose seat with a
difficult back corner

Examples of curves requiring snipping

CURVING BORDER STRIPS

When a fitted cover with borders is being cut and made up, the fullness on the borders can be reduced if necessary. The need for this often depends on the type of cover being used and on the shape of the work. Covers for chairs and stools with round seats, for example, can be better fitted by slightly curving the border pieces. On round seats, particularly stools with sloping sides, where the upholstery overhangs the frame, this technique is a good way of reducing fullness. Certainly, when hides and vinyl fabrics are used, cutting the borders in a gentle curve will take away unwanted fullness along the bottom tacking edges. This is an old practice which has always been followed in leatherwork, as leather can easily become overstretched.

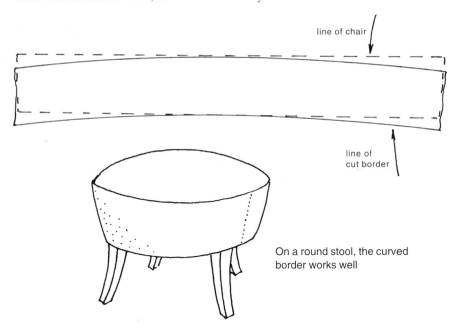

line of chair

line of cut border

On a round stool, the curved border works well

The curve on an average length of border for a small chair, say 600–750mm (24–30in), is about 38mm (1½in); shorter borders need less curve. If the borders are cut on the curve, rather than straight, the cover will hug and fit the chair shape very snugly when it is made up and pulled down for tacking.

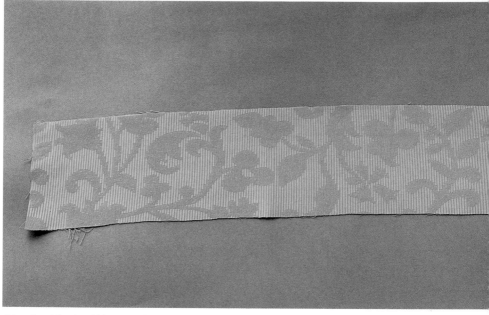

A border strip should be cut with a slight curve from end to end

The border after sewing

DISTORTED TAPESTRIES

Handmade tapestries produced on canvas and cotton scrim foundations, for stool and chair covers, will inevitably distort during stitching. Most pieces of work, unless you are very lucky, will pull out of shape, due to the tensions which build up with the stitching.

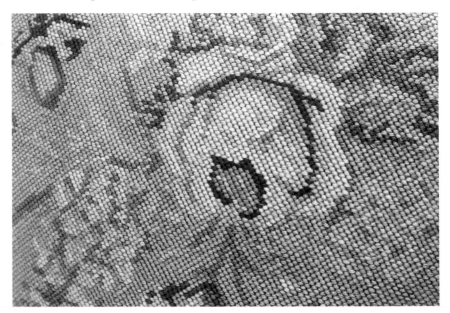

A tapestry showing some distortion

Before they can be used as covers, they need to be stretched and, at the same time, pulled back to their original square shape. When the distortion is very little, it is possible to reset them square during the upholstery process. However, it is best to assume that stretching and resetting prior to upholstery will be kinder to the work, and give better results.

The tapestry can be dealt with and drying out while a chair is being upholstered up to calico, ready for its cover. With the tapestry design face up, set the top edge of the canvas onto a large plywood board, well over the size of the tapestry. Temporary tack the first edge at 10mm (⅜in) intervals.

Soak a piece of white or neutral colour towelling in water and lay this on the board, under the tapestry, while it is still very wet. Bring the opposite bottom edge down over the towel, then slowly stretch and temporary tack it. Begin all the temporary tacking in the centre of the edges and work out to the ends. As tacking proceeds, line up the threads so that they are pulled beyond the vertical, in the opposite direction from the distortion. This allows for the canvas to relax a little when it is eventually removed.

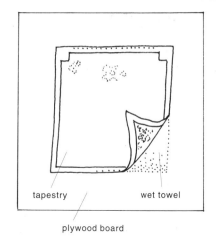

tapestry / wet towel

plywood board

Setting on over a wet towel

Now treat the two sides in the same way, stretching very firmly as the temporary tacks are fixed. It is likely that some of the tacking will need to be done twice in order to get the maximum stretch, a little at a time. Finish the mounting by completing the corners, which are normally left until last.

Check that the mounting and stretching is to your liking and then, using a fine, cold-water spray, wet the tapestry all over. Do this again 10 minutes later and leave it laid flat, not on end, to dry slowly for about 48 hours.

On some large pieces of tapestry or where the stitch work is multi-directional, the whole process may have to be repeated.

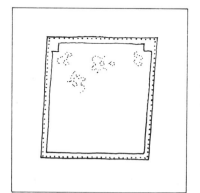

The tapestry, stretched and pulled, is held in place with tacks

DOUBLE PIPING

Double piping looks best on modern furniture or as a finish on a piece of reproduction work. For restoration work on antique and period pieces, the decoration and the finish should be kept to cords, braids and gimps, using the more traditional methods.

Double piping used to finish a reproduction chair

Using a wide strip of fabric, 75–88mm (3–3½in) wide, and two lengths of piping cord, as illustrated opposite, double piping can be made on the sewing machine, with a double-piping foot. The extra width gives more fabric to grip while feeding and controlling the tightness.

A double piping gives a neat and clean finish to a trimmed fabric edge, particularly against show-wood. Use a matching thread for the sewing, or a transparent polyester or nylon.

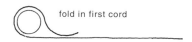
fold in first cord

position the second cord

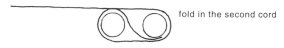
fold in the second cord

sew to fix the cords in place

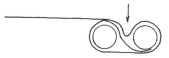

turn over and sew again, then trim

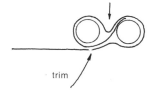

trim

Making double piping

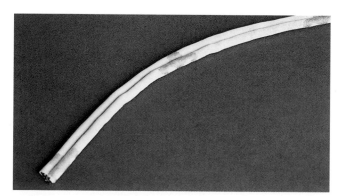

A length of double
piping after sewing
and trimming

EDGE DESIGN AND DETAIL

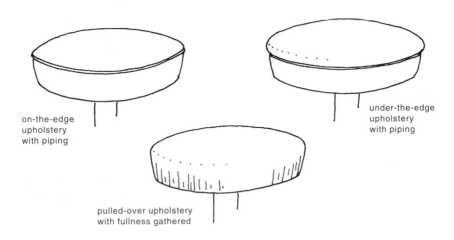

on-the-edge
upholstery
with piping

under-the-edge
upholstery
with piping

pulled-over upholstery
with fullness gathered

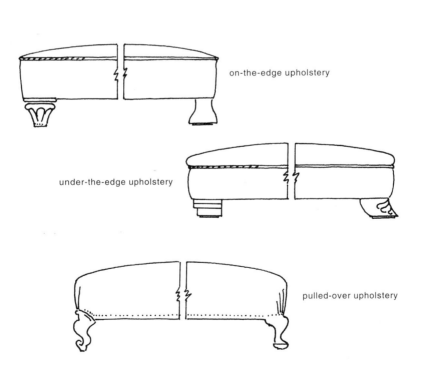

on-the-edge upholstery

under-the-edge upholstery

pulled-over upholstery

The three main options for the treatment of edges

'On-the-edge', 'under-the-edge', and 'pulled-over' are the three main options in upholstery for the treatment of edges. All three are quite distinct in appearance and will give a piece of work a completely different look. Fixing or stitching a cover 'on-the-edge' or 'under-the-edge' both require the addition of borders or a facing to complete the work. 'Pulling over' is a relatively simple treatment, and requires no further finishing.

Making the choice is a matter of creating the right detail for the individual piece. On certain types of work, such detail will often be decided for us historically. An incorrect choice will show up immediately when, sometimes for economic reasons, a fabric has been pulled over an edge rather than finished on the edge. However, in many situations any of the three types of edge will suffice.

the seat of a prie-dieu with on-the-edge upholstery, c.1840

a chesterfield settee with under-the-edge upholstery on the seat front, c.1915

an oak armchair with pull-over seat upholstery, c.1900

Particular styles of furniture dictate the edge detail

The construction of an upholstered edge on a seat, back or arm will also influence the finish and choice of detail. A traditional sprung edge, for example, will usually have an under-edge treatment. A seat with a very sharp and firm stitched edge is well suited to on-the-edge finishing with a border. The same edge, however, can be treated by pulling over and will look equally acceptable.

If you want to present your work in the best way, particularly traditional work, then the style or period of a piece should be allowed to influence the choice that you make. Take a look at period furniture illustrated in dictionaries of eighteenth- and nineteenth-century furniture. Research will generally indicate fairly accurately the original design features on chairs, settees and other pieces.

A visit to a museum or a stately home is also a good way of confirming exact upholstery detail. Museum pieces, in particular, will have either original upholstery on view or very accurate replicas. Trimmings and decorative finishes are equally important in traditional work and are worth noting. The edge design and trimmings will be complementary, relating to each other and to the mode of a particular period in time.

EDGE ROLLS: PLAIN AND TWIST

In traditional upholstery, the sock method is used to create roll edges on chair frames. The roll, which is made in the form of a stuffed sock, can be a plain, twist or tuft design. In fact, there is no limit to the variations possible. The most common edges are plain or twist styles. The twist produces a rope effect and is corded to accentuate and hold the design shape.

In England and France, from about 1850, fancy roll edges were used in upholstery – particularly on chairs – to create a style and accentuate the outlines of different types of seating. There were many variations which continued throughout the Victorian and into the Edwardian era. The later designs were often tufted or buttoned.

To prepare the roll in scrim, calico or ticking, cut a strip 250mm (10in) wide and machine sew the two edges to make a long sock. Stuff this sock with

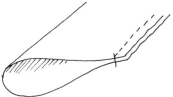

Fold and sew the scrim

A length of linen scrim sewn up into a sock

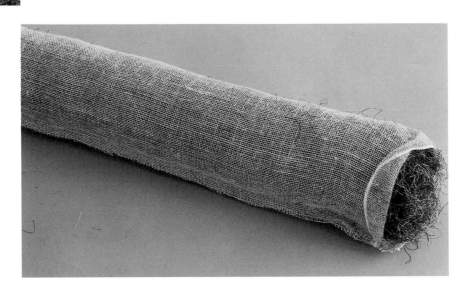

The scrim sock filled with curled hair

curled hair to the density required – 400g (14oz) of hair will produce an average size roll edge, 1m (3ft) long. With the seam on the underside, press the roll onto the frame edge and temporary tack it along each side, catching the cloth about every 25mm (1in).

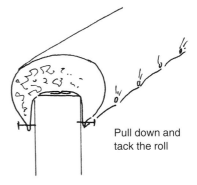

Pull down and tack the roll

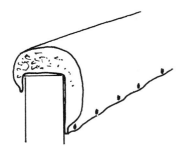

An alternative shape

At this stage the roll can be made as firm as may be required, depending on the type of design chosen. Use a regulator to smooth and even out the stuffing, or to create a roll-over effect, as illustrated above.

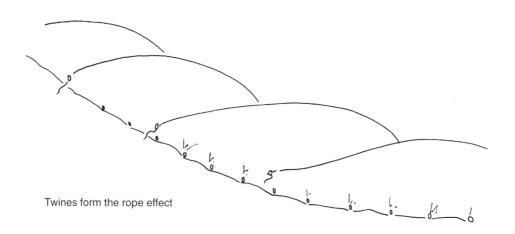

Twines form the rope effect

To produce the twist, or rope edges, as they are sometimes called, tack and pull lengths of twine over the surface at an angle to the roll. At the same time, move the stuffing away from each twine line, using the regulator, so that channels are made as the twines are tightened down.

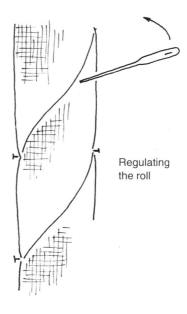

Regulating the roll

Apply the second or top stuffing of felt or wadding before fitting the covering. Lay the top stuffing carefully over the roll in strips, in order to maintain the channel shapes. Fit upholstery cords into each channel as you proceed.

FABRIC GIMP

It is possible to make a simple gimp trimming with narrow strips of upholstery fabric – a handmade replacement for what would usually be a bought gimp or braid. This can then be glued along a chair edge to finish the upholstery and cover the tacking, or used just for decoration.

Cut the strips 30mm (1¼in) wide and fold over the fabric. This fold should be overlapped for thin fabrics and butted for heavy covers: an overlap fold produces three thicknesses and a butt fold only two (see right). The length of the strip will depend on the amount required; gathering the strip after the stitching is complete will reduce the length by half. Press the folded strip with a hot iron set to suit the fabric type. This will set the folds and make the strip very flat.

After folding and pressing, the strip will be 12–15mm (½–⁹⁄₁₆in) wide. To produce the gimped effect, put a fine, close running stitch into the strip, working from one end. Seal the end of the thread by knotting or tying and commence stitching in a zigzag formation across the face of the strip (see right). Use a strong, matching sewing machine thread for the stitching.

The number of running stitches and the angle of the zigzag is a personal choice, and can be varied to give different effects. The samples shown were produced by working three stitches up and three stitches down, at an angle of about 45°. When gathered, the effect is very similar to a woven gimp.

Glue the gimp trimming in place with clear, tube glue, then turn the ends in and fix with gimp pins.

Making long lengths of this trimming would be very time-consuming, but it is well worth making a short strip for a small piece of upholstery and for single chairs and stools.

use a butting fold for heavier fabrics

use an overlapping fold for fine fabric

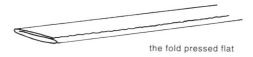

the fold pressed flat

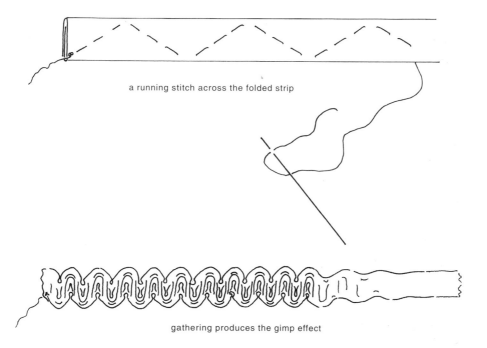

a running stitch across the folded strip

gathering produces the gimp effect

Making a gimp trimming

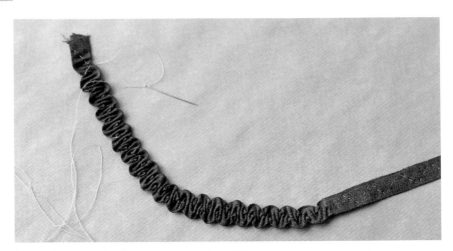

Use a strong machine thread for the running stitch

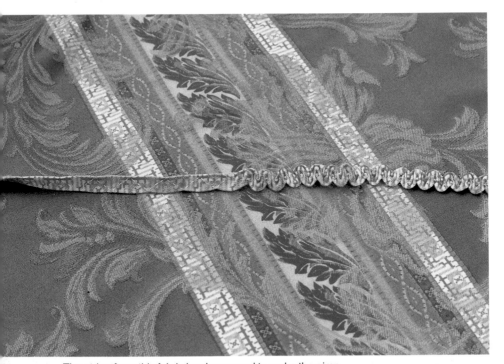

The stripe from this fabric has been used to make the gimp

FEATHER EDGE

A sharp and firm feather edge, also known as a welted edge, is used in upholstery when a good outline is required and a facing or border is going to be fixed to it. The feather-edge stitch is the final row of stitching applied to a ready-made edge. The ready-made edge will usually have a row of blind stitching and two rows of top stitching. To prepare the edge, regulate it with a small, fine-point regulator to ensure that the very tip of the scrim edge is well filled, and is already tight.

Two different, but equally effective methods can be used to make a feather edge: the English and the French. The English method uses a blanket stitch formation along the tip of the edge, while the French method uses a fine top stitch set very close to the tip of the scrim. The resulting edges of both are crisp, firm and sharp and will support any second stage upholstery which is fixed to them.

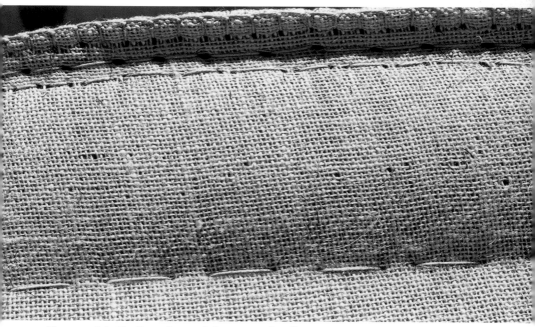

The completed feather edge ready for a second stuffing

The blanket stitch produces a sharp, fine edge

Feather-edge stitching will often be found on nineteenth-century pieces, for example, mock cushion seats, arms and back facings, and some stools or banquettes. The inside back upholstery on many French chairs will also have feathered edges.

A feather edge is made using a fine mattress twine and either a straight, two-point needle or a large circular needle. The stitch begins with a slip knot and proceeds along the edge either in a blanket formation, plain or knotted (the English method), or as a fine, knotted top stitch (the French method). Both formations have stitches which are about 20mm (¾in) long.

FEATHERS AND DOWN

Very thin, soft animal skins, such as goatskin, moleskin and chamois (shammy), were the materials traditionally used for featherproof cases. Skins are naturally proof and were sometimes made up with the fur of the animal on the inside of the case; this furry surface allowed the feathers and down to move. Loose fillings depend on flow and movement for comfort and to enable reshaping and plumping after use.

The town of Cambrai in northern France is where the fine cotton cloth called cambric originated. With their waxed and semi-glazed surface, finer cambrics are used to make featherproof cases for upholstery and bedding. Another fabric which has traditionally been used for this is mattress or Belgian ticking. It is woven twill and can be made feather- and downproof.

Today, cambric is the material principally used for proofed cushion cases. It is normally made from 100% cotton and the weave is extremely close. When cambric has a glazed surface, the glazed side is kept to the inside of the case, which aids movement of the fillings.

Cutting to size

Cambric interiors for feather and down cushions are cut larger than the finished cushion size. This ensures a well-filled cover with the filling reaching into the corners and curves. After allowances have been made for sewing, add 30mm (1¼in) to the width and the length of the cambric and 30mm (1¼in) to the height of the border.

Seat and back cushions for chairs are made with partitioning strips, so that the feathers are separated into compartments in the case. This keeps the filling well spread and holds it where it is needed most. Draw the division lines onto the main panels in pencil and sew the strips, which should always be 50mm (2in) higher than the borders, to each panel, along these lines.

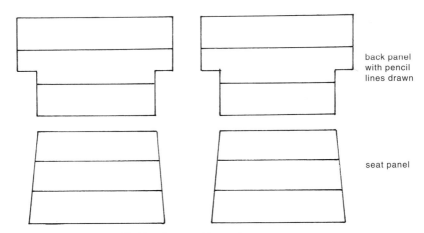

back panel
with pencil
lines drawn

seat panel

Marking the panel templates

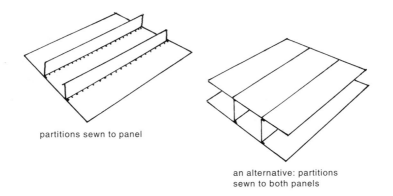

partitions sewn to panel

an alternative: partitions
sewn to both panels

Sewing the partitions in place

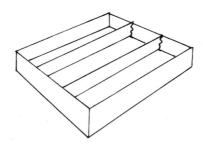

The borders sewn in

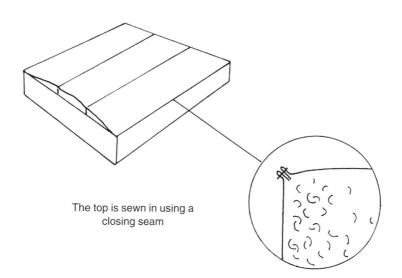

The top is sewn in using a
closing seam

The second stage of the assembly is to sew the borders to the first panel, all round the case. Finally, sew the second panel to the top edge of the borders, using a closing stitch seam, with each raw edge turned in and laid together. The closing seam should be about 5mm (¼in) in from the edge. Do not sew the ends of the division strips to the borders.

A bordered cushion of an average size for an armchair will use 1.6kg (3½lb) of feather. A bolster filled with 100% feather will need 700g per 300mm (1½lb per foot).

A unique advantage of feather and down fillings is that they are 'shake-up'; shaking them will plump them up and freshen them, restoring their shape after use. A very good blend of filling for upholstery purposes is 50/50 feather and down.

There is only one other cushion filling that has similar properties and that is a synthetic filling developed by ICI called Comforel. It is very soft, lightweight and slippery to the touch, and can be used as an alternative to feathers and down.

FIXING UPHOLSTERY

All upholstery fabrics have stretch; some have only a little, while others can have quite a lot. Some fabrics stretch more in the weft direction than in the warp. The construction or weave of a fabric will usually influence the way it responds to pulling and stretching.

To get the best results from most types of covering, temporary tacks are used to set a cover in place – the first fixing is seldom the final fixing in upholstery. This process allows a fabric to be worked in order to gradually stretch and tighten it over the shape to be covered, for a second fixing. The temporary tacks are very quickly removed with a swing of the hammer.

In most cases, begin tacking at the centre of an edge, and stretch out the fabric from the centre towards each corner as tacking proceeds. At the same time, pull the fabric over the rail and fix it in position. When all sides have been temporarily tacked and stretched outwards in this way, the cover will begin to feel taut and the

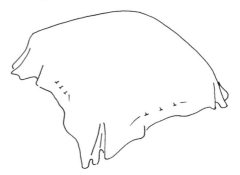

Setting the cover in place
with temporary tacks

upholstery will start to develop a good line. Brush and smooth the fabric firmly with the fingers and palm of your hand as you fix and refix the tacks.

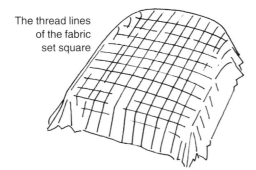

The thread lines
of the fabric
set square

The principles of working and tightening down a covering are the same whatever shape the frame may be. A circular seat and a D-shape seat are covered in exactly the same way as a more conventional square seat.

It is only the excess fabric that has to be worked over the frame and the resulting fullness that varies. In plan view, the weft and warp threads in the fabric will be the same. On shaped seats the thread lines will drift off evenly and will drop, often quite dramatically, at the corners.

Corners are usually dealt with last, when all of the main tacking and setting is done. This gives you the opportunity to work out fullness, and gather or pleat where necessary. Setting the corners in place will also allow you some final stretching to take small amounts of wrinkle, created by smoothing with your hands, out and over the corners.

Tension and improve the edge lines of the upholstery with good fixings at the corners. You can then put temporary tacks in between the previous tacks as you even out any dips or tack bites. All tacks can then be hammered in; again, leave the corners until last.

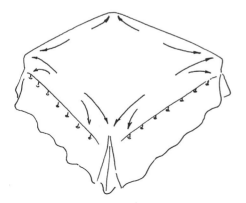

Pulling towards the corners to
stretch out the cover

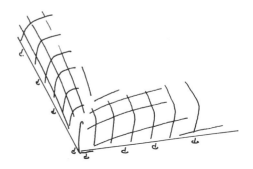

Corners pulled hard,
pleated and tacked

FIXING WEBBINGS

In upholstered furniture, good strong fixings for webbings are a basic essential. A whole seat or back in a chair will depend on the web foundation for many years of use. To produce the strongest foundations, the following rules have to be followed.

To begin with, the end of a webbing should never be turned in; it should always be turned uppermost so that it provides a flap or washer under the heads of the tacks. This protects the main web from the tack heads and increases the clamping action of the tacks.

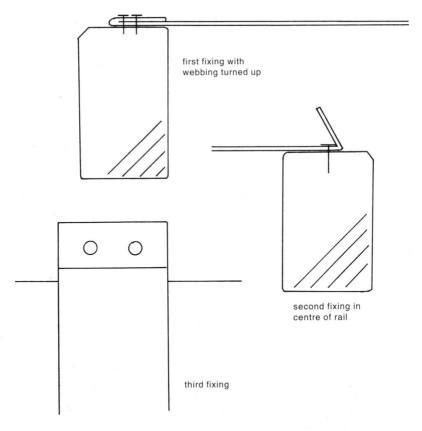

first fixing with
webbing turned up

second fixing in
centre of rail

third fixing

When fixing, the edge of the webbing should always be turned up

All inner rail edges should have their sharp edges removed, before webbing is fitted, so that chafing to the webbings does not occur.

Using enough tacks of the correct size is the next consideration. The large heads of improved tacks give the best fixing. Using them is a good rule for seats, but they may sometimes be too heavy for fine work on delicate frames. In some cases, when the timber is old, brittle and delicate, or when new timber is used, fine tacks will be more suitable.

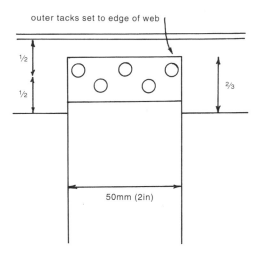

Tacks arranged in a dogtrot formation

For general webbing work, five tacks at each end of a web is the minimum. These should be arranged in a 'dogtrot' (zigzag) formation and not in a straight line, or there is a risk of splitting

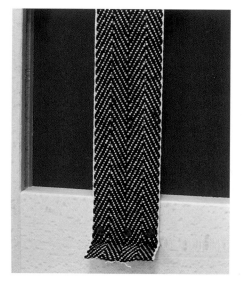

▲ The first fixing with outer tacks close to the edge of the web

◄ The second fixing after stretching tight

in a rail. A dogtrot is also a strong formation for the webbing weave. The positioning of webs is important, and the line of the tacks should be as near to the centre of the rail as possible: too near the outer edge and they are likely to be seen, and to cause an uneven line for the coverings; too near the inner edge and they may cause breakout of the timber when the webs are strained very tightly. Another golden rule is that the outer tacks in a line of five or more must be close to the edge of each web. This ensures that the webbing edge is taut and does not curl when stretched.

Webs are tacked under the rails for sprung upholstery, and on the rail for top-stuffed, unsprung work, though there are some instances when this will not be the case. On chair backs, for example, the webs may be on the rail or at the back, depending on the depth of springing required. In addition, on some deep-seated chairs, the seat webs can be tacked on top of the main rails to avoid the need for very deep seat springs, which are wasteful and costly and, today, considered unnecessary.

Black-and-white webbings, interwoven to form a good formation

FLANGING A CORD

With a piping foot fitted to the sewing machine, a trimming cord can be flanged to make sewing in and fixing easier. The machine foot should have a groove of about 6mm (¼in) or more to accommodate the cord.

The downward pressure of the foot should be reset to light pressure only, with enough for positive feeding.

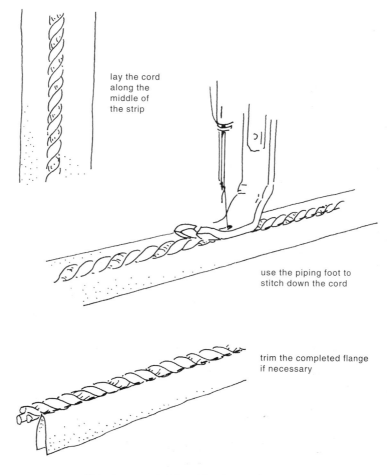

lay the cord along the middle of the strip

use the piping foot to stitch down the cord

trim the completed flange if necessary

Flanging an upholstery trimming cord

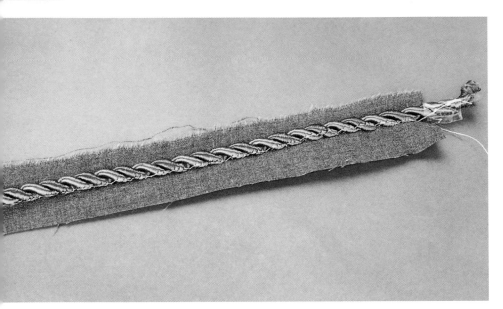

The stitch line catches the edge of the cord

Begin by cutting a strip of cotton lining cloth of a neutral or matching colour. The strips can be 38–50mm (1½in–2in) wide and will be trimmed down after sewing. Lay the flange strip under the needle, then lay the cord over this strip, down the centre. Now lower the piping foot onto the cord and check that the cord is well to the left of the needle. The needle should be just catching the edge of the cord, with the stitch line running along the centre of the strip.

Try a few inches of sewing, then stop to check that the cord is being caught by the stitch and that the flange strip is not puckering. It may be necessary to hold the flange and the cord taut, with both hands moving forward at the same rate as the feed. The sewing speed needs to be gentle and steady. An ideal stitch length for this job is three stitches per cm (eight stitches per inch).

Fold the flange double at the sewing line and check that the cord has been caught regularly; it is not necessary that every stitch should catch. The folded flange can now be trimmed to an even width, ready for use.

A flanged cord is useful for sewing into cushion covers and fitted covers, and of course, it can be tacked or stapled to frame edges and borders. For stitching in by hand around facings and edges, a flange will also speed up the trimming process.

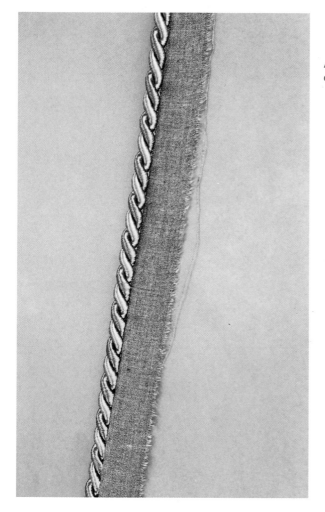

A length of flanged
cord ready for use

FLY PIECES

A fly is an extension to the main cover in upholstery, and may be optional or fitted to create shape. Flies are often used to save on cover fabric; they can save as much as 500mm (20in) or more in some cases. At tuckaway points on a chair, an odd strip of waste can be sewn on for economy. A fly piece can also be used to create a pull-in when sewn at a point on the reverse of a fabric. It can then be stitched or tacked to hold a shape and form a line in the upholstery design.

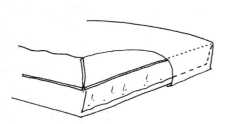

Securing a border with a fly

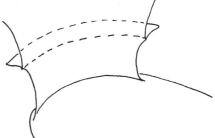

A fly used as a pull-in

Generally, flies are straight strips of fabric, but occasionally there is a need to shape a fly. Alternatively, a fly strip can be gathered along the sewing line to create spread and allow shaping to be produced, similar to a skirt.

Gathered and shaped flies will usually be cut from the same covering as the chair, as they are sewn along the base of an inside arm or back and may be visible.

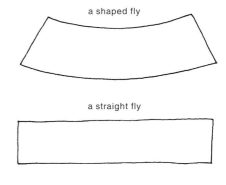

a shaped fly

a straight fly

a gathered fly

Examples of flies

A hessian fly piece machine sewn along the base of a cover panel

The tub chair offers a very good example of a fly being fitted to function as a shaping strip, in this case it is usually fitted along the curve of the inside arms and inside back. In this case, the flies are doing the same job as a gusset.

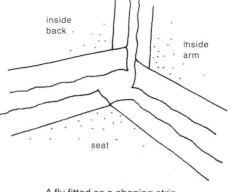

inside back

inside arm

seat

A fly fitted as a shaping strip

FOAM FILLINGS

To get good results with upholstery foams they must be understood. As with any filling used for upholstery, it is essential to know how it can best be worked and what its limitations are. Where and how to cut it, how much it can be stretched, and how it reacts to contact glues are some of the important considerations when using cellular urethane foams.

In basic terms, there are five different grades of hardness; very soft, soft, medium, firm, and very firm. Density and cost also affect performance, but they are not under consideration here. However, chip foams or reconstituted foams are all high density and are firm or very firm.

Most foam manufacturers will welcome enquiries and are quite happy to supply a guide on the use of their foams. For pillows, cushions and wraps, use very soft foam. For inside backs use soft foam, and for lumbar areas use medium. For seats use medium and firm foam together. For edgings, insulators and platforms, use very firm. This is a very general guide – when it is economical to do so, combinations of two or three hardnesses can be laminated to get the right feel and the best service from the product.

Most foam elements in upholstery are fabricated pieces, held together with foam adhesive. Shaping and fabrication together with gluing techniques will combine to give satisfactory results. Some useful examples are shown.

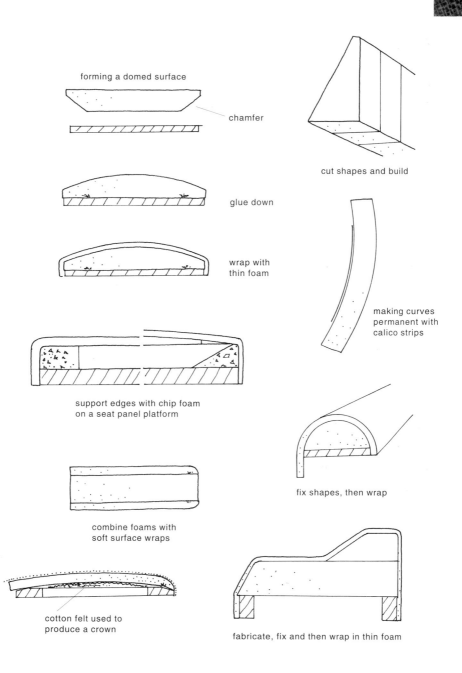

forming a domed surface

chamfer

glue down

wrap with
thin foam

support edges with chip foam
on a seat panel platform

combine foams with
soft surface wraps

cotton felt used to
produce a crown

cut shapes and build

making curves
permanent with
calico strips

fix shapes, then wrap

fabricate, fix and then wrap in thin foam

Shaping and fabricating foam elements

GAINSBOROUGH ARM CUTS

The eighteenth-century, Gainsborough-style chair, with long arm supports each side of the seat, presents a cover cutting challenge. A series of five careful cuts around the upright is needed to bring the two cut edges of the first cut back together. If cut well, these two edges will butt together. They can then be gimp pinned before the cover is finished with upholstery nails or a braid. With some thought, and careful manipulating and trimming, a good cut is easier to achieve than it would first appear.

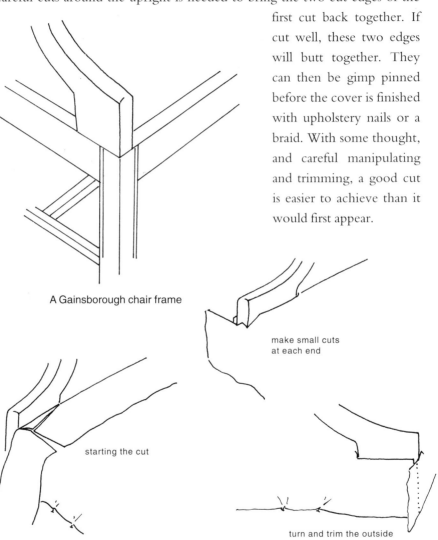

A Gainsborough chair frame

make small cuts at each end

starting the cut

turn and trim the outside

Cutting around the arm supports

There are two positions for arm stumps of this type. The Gainsborough chair, which is a mid-eighteenth-century piece, has a curving support for the arms which ends at the front of the seat. Where it meets the seat side rails, the arm stump may be as long as 125–150mm (5–6in), and this has to be cut around to reproduce the upholstery design in its traditional style. The other type of support has an arm upright of less width and is set back a little from the seat front. The cuts for each type are similar; practise them with calico before attempting them in an expensive covering. After cutting, turn all the raw edges in and tuck them away around the arm stump.

Upholstery nails are typical of the finish used for this period for both leather and fabric coverings.

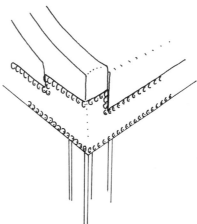

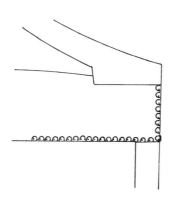

Finishing with brass nails

An alternative method, using a
nailed border

GATHERING FABRICS AND COVERS

Gathering, like pleating or folding, is a way of reducing and shaping a flat material. By gathering, we make a covering of any type conform to the shape that we want. Less formal than folding or pleating, gathering allows a fabric to sit easily on a surface and to go where it naturally wants to, rather than stretching it and forcing it to conform. It is a form of tailoring used continually by the upholsterer. There are many variations, but the four most common methods will give you a wide choice for use on most applications.

The obvious choice for fixed upholstery is to gather by hand and work the fabric with random gathering and tacking.

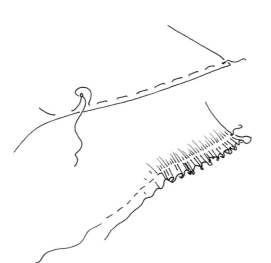

Gathering and tacking by hand

Gathering with a running stitch

A second method, used in soft furnishing and upholstery, is to gather on a thread or twine or, in some cases, on a wire. Using a needle to produce a running stitch or an overedge stitch is a very common and well used method of producing a gather. It is the usual choice when gathering is to be featured as a decorative effect, for example, a gathered or ruched border on a chair. Once the fabric has been gathered, fix and hold it

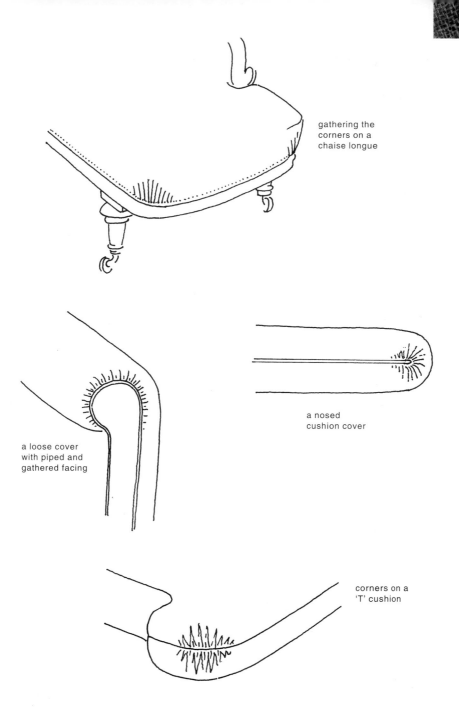

gathering the
corners on a
chaise longue

a loose cover
with piped and
gathered facing

a nosed
cushion cover

corners on a
'T' cushion

Examples of tailoring where gathering is commonly used

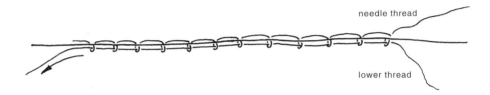

A long, loose stitch using the sewing machine

by hand stitching to an edge to make it permanent. If you prefer, use the sewing machine to put a thread into the fabric, prior to gathering. The stitch length should be set to the largest stitch on the machine and the needle thread tension reduced so that the stitch formed is a loose one. The fabric can then be drawn up and gathered by pulling the bottom or under thread.

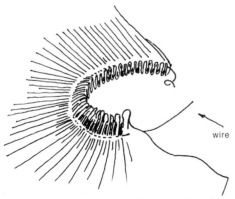

For large amounts of fabric, gather the fabric on a wire

Working on a much greater scale, to gather the large amounts of fabric required for tented ceilings and four-poster beds, a wire is used. The fabric edge is pierced with this wire in order to keep it firm and hold it at a centre point. Once the fabric has been gathered and tightened, the wire is fixed into a

A tented ceiling with the fabric gathered on a central circle of wire

circle by twisting. It can then be permanently fixed at a chosen point on the ceiling, or above the bed. This fixing is usually completed with wire staples or very strong twine.

Using a short strip of elastic to gather the corner of a fabric is another very effective method. Predetermine the amount or length of the gathering, and mark the start and finish with a notch or with chalk. Cut a piece of strong, 10mm (⅜in) elastic to the length of the finished gather, then stretch this out to reach the marks, and machine sew it in place while it is stretched. It helps if you pin the elastic at each mark as you do this stretching and sewing. As the elastic is allowed to relax, after sewing, it will gather the fabric evenly to a pre-marked length. In cushion making, for example, the gathering is then made permanent by sewing it onto the second, opposite piece.

Using strong elastic to gather a pre-set length

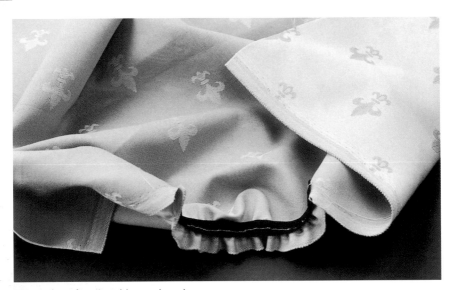

The gather after stretching and sewing

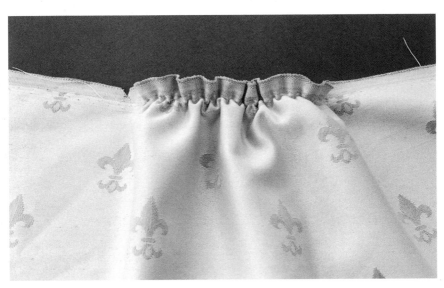

The finished gather ready for making up

The effects of gathering and ruching on plain fabrics, such as velvets and silks, is very distinct and very attractive. On busy, patterned fabrics they are less obvious, but in a practical sense, equally useful.

GAUGES

Sewing and knitting gauges are a very useful part of the upholsterer's tool kit. In addition, a pair of dividers, which can be adjusted to set distances, will be handy on the cutting table when covers are being marked out. Repeat measurements, and marking out spacing in fluting and buttoning, for example, are two instances when the dividers will help with accuracy and speed up the work.

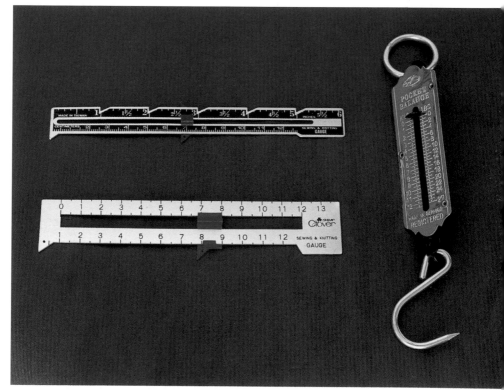

Adjustable gauges and a spring balance

On the workbench, a small gauge has numerous uses; those sold for sewing and knitting are ideal for upholstery work. They are low cost, simple to use and quickly adjusted for measuring and checking precise work.

Checking the height of a stitched edge

Stitched edges need to be checked for height, especially when sets of chairs are being upholstered: the sofa seats or backs, or the two opposite sides of a chair, must be kept the same if the upholstery is to look balanced.

Some gauges are notched with centres set in inch or centimetre spaces. These can be very useful when accurate spacing is wanted and the notched measurements can be taken off quickly.

GLOSSARY: DID YOU KNOW?

Early in the eighteenth century, many household accounts show the name **Appolstoror**, as the person who carried out upholstery work.

A **bag of walnuts** was the term often used to describe a badly done piece of upholstery in the 1930s and 1940s. Apprentices were often accused of producing this when their first attempts at upholstery proved difficult.

In the furniture trade workshops of the 1950s, **Bill Spokeshave** was the name used when the work of William Shakespeare was being discussed.

In the mid-eighteenth century several new designs of **couch**, introduced from France, had the grand names of **Sultane**, **Ottomane** and **Turquoise**. There was a demand at the time for new fashion in the furnishing of homes for the rich.

From the early part of the twentieth century, the term **dogtrot** was used to describe the zigzag arrangement of tacks in webbings.

Three names commonly used to describe **Edwardian couches** were **Cromwell**, **Drumhead**, and **Bolster arm**. All were very typical designs of the period and commonly called **parlour couches**.

The invention of the modern sewing machine is often credited to **Elias Howe**. In 1853, he sued all the machine manufacturers in the United States, claiming that their machines were derived from his prototype, patented in 1847. He won his case, was awarded a royalty of $25 per machine, and became rich overnight.

A **fenderette** was a long, low stool made from oak or mahogany, which stood in front of an open fire. They were used to warm the feet and were usually covered in Morocco or roan goatskin leathers. The corner joints of the frame were reinforced with nailed copper plates.

The apostle and great traveller, **St Paul**, was by trade a tent maker. He is regarded as the Patron Saint of upholsterers. The coat of arms of the Upholders Company is a shield with three tents emblazoned.

In 1910, **pom-poms** were used to ornament upholsterers' work. To make pom-poms, wind yarns around two spikes, set 600mm (12in) apart, to a good thickness and tie off at 38mm (1½in) intervals. Cut off halfway between each tie to make eight pom-poms. You can give a pom-pom a vandyked edge by trimming it with a mattress-tuft punch or pinking shears.

Upholstery edged with pom-poms

In 1474, The Upholders Company of the City of London presented a petition to the Lord Mayor in which it was reported that 'thistledown, cats tails and horse hair' were all being used 'as **stuffings for bedding**' (Corporation of London Record Office, Karin M Walton).

Tack bites is the term used in upholstery to describe an uneven edge or a series of lines caused by the pulls from tacking. This is often apparent when fine, lustrous fabrics are being used, such as silks.

The **treadle sewing machine**, invented in the United States in the 1850s, had the big advantage of leaving both hands free to control the cloth. However, in Britain it was regarded with great suspicion until the twentieth century. The action was considered unladylike and harmful to the ankles.

A wooden **web strainer** with two slots was in common use at the very beginning of the twentieth century. It was gradually superseded by the peg-type strainer, which remains a favourite today.

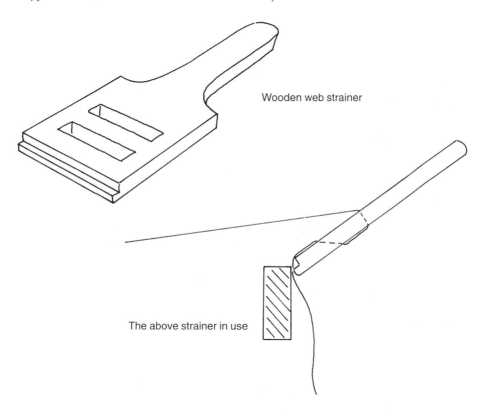

Wooden web strainer

The above strainer in use

References to upholders and their duties of upholding and providing furnishings can be found dating from 1294. **The Worshipful Company of Upholders** received the grant of its Coat of Arms in 1465 and a Royal Charter in 1626. The Royal Charter was confirmed by Charles II in 1668 after the destruction of the original in the Great Fire of 1666.

GUSSETS

In the Oxford dictionary a gusset is described as a piece let into a garment to strengthen or enlarge a part. In much earlier times, a 'gousset' was a piece filling up a joint in armour. It certainly has its uses in upholstery; in fact, anywhere a cover has to be spread and cut at a difficult corner, or where it is necessary to reinforce a cut near to the surface of the work, as shown in the two examples.

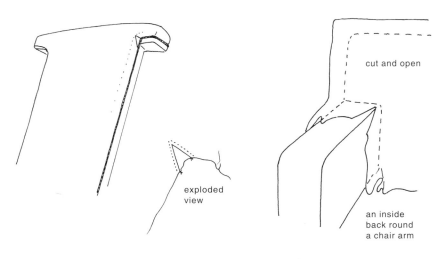

exploded view

cut and open

an inside back round a chair arm

A gusset can be used on a prie-dieu chair

Cutting the fabric to find the gusset size required

To make the gusset fit the fabric at the point to be gusseted, pin or temporary tack the fabric in place, then carefully make a cut to release the fabric, and allow the cut to open as much as it needs to. This allows the cover to sit well into place and indicates how large the gusset piece should be.

Cut out the gusset shape and test it for size, then trim if necessary. It is often best to cut the gusset on the cross or the bias of the fabric: this gives a little more flexibility, and makes a neater job. Now remove the cover from the work and sew the gusset by machining it down one side of the cut, across the

A gusset trimmed and ready for sewing into the cut panel

Sewing in the gusset piece

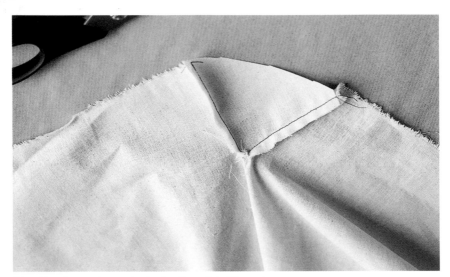

Checking the sewing and snipping the point of the cut

The finished gusset, in place

point of the cut, then out along the second edge. The fitted gusset will sit neatly into the corner as the cover is tacked and tightened into place. Some careful snipping may be needed at the point of the cut to allow it to flatten, and to release any fabric tension.

HAIR STUFFING TECHNIQUES

The craft of edge stuffing using curled hair and scrim is a very old and traditional skill which has developed over the last 200 years so that today we are able to benefit from the honed techniques that were gradually improved by our predecessors.

Getting enough stuffing, curled hair or vegetable fibres into an edge on a chair frame is always a problem, especially to novice upholsterers. An edge can only be created by feel, using your hands and the scrim covering to squeeze and stuff the correct amount into place. Bridle twines or stuffing ties are an essential part of the process and allow us to control and build the density of the filling. There are two methods which I use, and both have helped me with the forming of stuffed edges, giving a control over the stuffing which allows me to build the type of edge I choose for different kinds of work.

Method 1: using the bridles to gain density

In the first method the ties are used as a control, as small handfuls of hair or fibre are slid under and pushed along a loop. Up to four, and sometimes as many as six small amounts are pushed along under one tie. This builds a density of stuffing before moving on to the next tie, and so on. Finally, a loose, even layer may be needed all along the edge before the scrim is pulled over, to test its feel and strength.

Method 1: sliding small handfuls of hair along the ties to gain density

handful of hair   twist   nose

tail

Method 2: twisting and folding the hair

The second method is used mainly with animal hair, because it produces fairly firm bunches of the filling. Begin by putting the ties in place, then take a small handful of hair, form it into a long slither and give it a twist, using both hands, to form what feels like a loose rope. Fold this twist in half to produce what is called a 'nose and tail'. Slide the nose or folded end under the tie, with the nose to the front of the edge. As many as three noses will be

Method 2: twisting the hair before folding

needed to fill each tie. The edge will feel quite firm already, with the noses lined up along the rail edge and the tails towards the centre of the seat. The line of noses now needs to be teased out so that they blend together.

The rest of the seat should be stuffed less firmly, either by using the first method or by making much softer nose and tail bunches. If you use nose and tail bunches, these should be placed in the centre of the seat, with the noses down and the softer tails uppermost, before being teased out as for the edges. Once again, it may sometimes be necessary to produce a smoother surface by adding a soft, loose layer over the seat and edges before adding the scrim.

Tacking the scrim covering in place

When the scrim covering and tacking is complete, you will notice how firm the edges become as soon as one or two rows of blind stitching are put in. The stuffing technique you select should always be influenced by the type of edge required, its height and the period of the piece being worked on.

HEALTH AND SAFETY

Like many crafts, upholstery is quite a physical activity. It is therefore worth a few moments to consider your health and safety when you are working. Noise and physical strain are two things which are unavoidable in a workshop environment, but they do need to be kept to the minimum if you are to enjoy your work and continue to work for any length of time.

Noise

The hammer, the staple gun and most power tools produce noise levels which, after a time, can damage hearing. In upholstery, we have to work close to all of these tools and though it will not initially be noticeable, the noise created can, after a while, begin to affect the ear's delicate mechanisms. It is impossible to exclude noise but we can take steps to reduce it as much as possible. If you can, avoid working in confined spaces, such as small rooms with low ceilings. Have a door or a window open to make your workspace as large as possible and insulate or pad your work surface or bench, if only with an old blanket or a piece of carpet or underlay.

A padded bench and a mallet covered with hide

Think of ways in which you can reduce or dampen noise in the workshop. You can cover the face of a wooden mallet, for example, by gluing or stapling on a piece of thick hide. This reduces the noise produced and at the same time helps to preserve the face of the mallet and the handle of the ripping chisel. Tough rubber or composite flooring or matting will help stop noise travelling round a workroom and heavy fabric draped on a wall or at a window will also absorb noise.

Strain

As a beginner in the trade, I soon learnt from my elder workmates that a day's work at the bench could be quite tiring. I was told that moving the work rather than moving myself was always much better. It isn't necessary to stand on your head to complete the upholstery of a chair. Working in the right sequence and, for example, moving a chair onto its side or back, can reduce your own need to move drastically. You can soon get into the habit of leaving some areas of the work temporary tacked until later, when the chair is turned over, which again, reduces bending and awkward working.

As work proceeds, a piece of upholstery gets heavier, particularly traditional or antique pieces and, of course, settees and the like.

I have noticed that old pictures and drawings from eighteenth-century books and essays that describe the upholsterer's work, nearly always illustrate the upholsterer in a sitting position. Personally, I find it difficult to work on the floor squatting over a piece. However, there are times when work can be much more comfortably done when sitting. Loose seats are a good example, provided a low table or benchboard is set close to you for support. Some stitchwork and finishing work is also often done more comfortably from a stool, rather than standing over the work. No doubt, you will find your own best way of working comfortably, which very often means more quickly.

Back strain is generally reckoned to be the most common problem associated with upholstery, with hands and wrists coming a close second. By nature, the work needs to be pulled, stretched and made tight before fixing – keep your arms relaxed and use your body weight for stretching materials. It is important that we take this aspect of our craft seriously, so that it can be enjoyed and found more rewarding.

HESSIANS AND SCRIMS

Hessian is a plain weave fabric with 12 ends (horizontal yarns) and 13 picks (vertical yarns) per inch. It is made from coarse jute yarns which are the same for warp and weft so that it can be used in either direction. The cloth is very fibrous and made in a variety of weights; 7½, 10, 12 and 14oz per sq yd (210, 280, 340 and 400g per 900mm sq).

A 14oz (400g) hessian is known as 'tarpaulin' and is very heavy. The 12oz (340g) weight is a good, strong hessian for upholstery work, particularly over springs of any type. It is a robust cloth and will withstand the wear and tear created by the movement of springs in use.

A 10oz (280g) hessian is a good general-purpose weight, and is ideal for unsprung areas on arms, backs and small seats. The lightest 7½oz (210g) hessian used in upholstery resembles a loosely woven, poor-quality scrim. Its uses are very limited, except when a good scrim is not available or when it can be used to support and line the outside covers on chairs.

Scrim is the loose weave cloth used to cover first stuffings in traditional upholstery. It is made from jute or linen yarn. Both jute and linen scrim are approximately 8–9oz (220–235g) weight, with linen being the finer cloth of the two, and generally more expensive. Choose a linen scrim for fine, good-quality work: it is softer to the touch and it works and shapes well.

Left to right: Two grades of hessian, 12 and 10oz (340 and 280g), jute scrim and linen scrim

HOLE COLLARS

Using a hole collar is a way of making a non-fray hole in an upholstery fabric to fit round a protruding dowel peg or over a dowel hole. Occasionally, in modern upholstery, a tubular steel upright emerging through a seat will need a similar treatment. This simple technique is worth having up your sleeve for when the odd occasion arises.

An example I came across recently was on an interesting chaise longue which had a removable backrest. The rest could be unscrewed and the seat cushion turned over so that the backrest could be slotted in on the other side. This meant that the chaise longue could easily be converted from a left-hand to a right-hand piece.

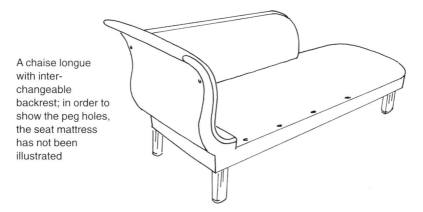

A chaise longue with inter-changeable backrest; in order to show the peg holes, the seat mattress has not been illustrated

The four holes along each side of the seat frame had to have openings in the platform cover to accommodate the pegs on the base of the backrest. The holes were accurately marked on the platform cover, and a small collar was sewn into each hole.

To fit a collar into a small hole, carefully mark the position of the hole on the face side of the main covering. Cut a small square of the same fabric for the collar piece, about four times larger than the hole; if the hole required is 25mm (1in) across, the collar piece should be about 100mm (4in) square.

Locate this square face down and centred over the mark, then pin it in place with several pins and mark the outline of the hole onto the collar piece. Whether the hole is round, square or whatever shape, machine sew around the outline marked, using a close stitch. With the outline sewn, cut away the centre of the hole, through both plies, leaving a small seam allowance of 6mm (¼in). Remove all the pins so that the collar piece can be pushed completely through the hole and formed flat on the underside of the fabric. To keep it in place, the collar may need pressing or spot gluing on the underside of the main cover. The result is a clean, neat hole with the collar just visible at the edges. If the hole distorts or will not lay flat, it can be very gently hammered around the edges, and it may help to snip the seam allowance with a fine pair of scissors, just up to the sewing line. This will release any tension created by turning the collar.

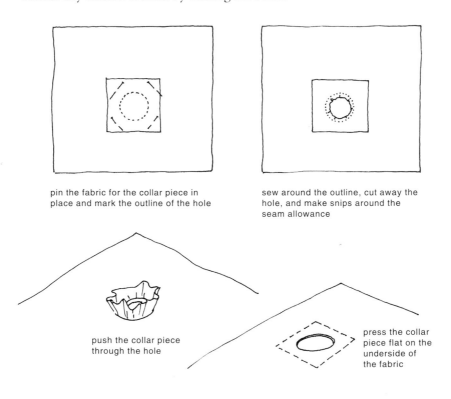

pin the fabric for the collar piece in place and mark the outline of the hole

sew around the outline, cut away the hole, and make snips around the seam allowance

push the collar piece through the hole

press the collar piece flat on the underside of the fabric

Fitting a collar into a hole

JOINS FOR PIPING

The scarf join and the skived join are just two of the many joins used to finish and lengthen pipings. They are very different joins, used in two quite different situations. The overlapping scarf join is mainly a join for soft covers, whereas the skived join is a glued join used for pipings made in hide.

a scarf join used to finish piping

a skived join to finish leather

A comparison of scarf and skived joins

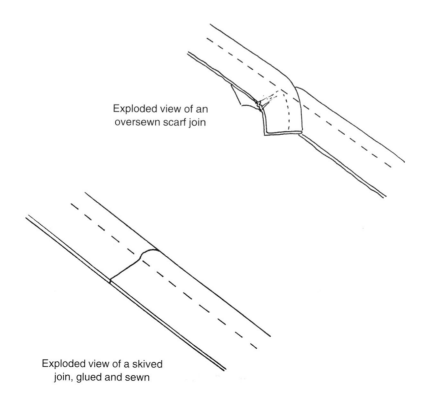

Exploded view of an oversewn scarf join

Exploded view of a skived join, glued and sewn

Pipings trimmed to a 25mm (1in) overlap

To finish the piping of a fabric cushion cover, trim the two ends so that they overlap by 25mm (1in), then take out and trim the piping cords so that they do not overlap. Lay the two ends one on top of the other so that they run off the sewing line, at an angle, in a sandwich form. Hold the two in place while machining straight across the join. This will form a diagonal scarf line well suited to piping, especially if it has been bias cut.

The angled scarf join after sewing

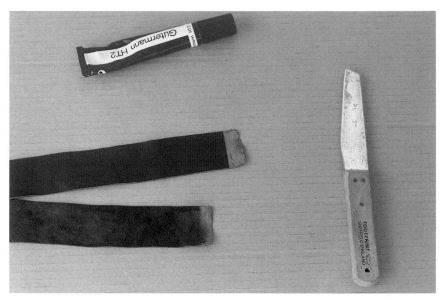

Skiving the leather strips to a paper-thin edge

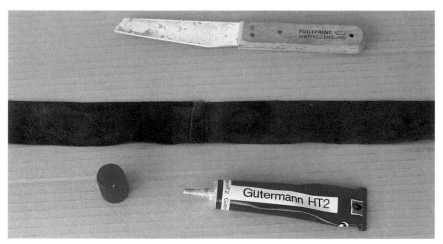

The join glued, ready for sewing

A skived join in leather piping is prepared by shaving or skiving the two ends of piping strip to be joined. With a sharp, straight-blade knife, make an angled shaving cut from the face side of one piece and from the reverse side of the other. Cut each to a fine, paper-thin edge, then glue them together with a contact adhesive so that the skived edges overlap. This should produce an almost invisible join in leather piping. Take care not to allow glue onto the surface of the hide. Machine across the join to finish, with the overlapping skiver towards you so that the cut edge is not lifted by the machine foot.

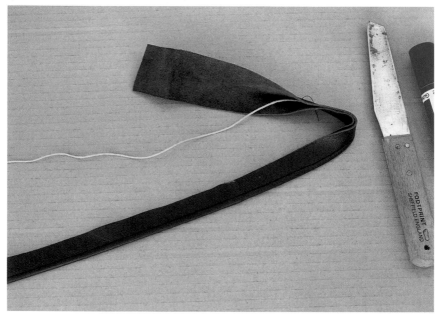

The completed piping strip – upholstery twine can be used to produce fine pipings in hide

JOINT LINES

To get a true, even line for a sewing joint on curved backs, arms or seats, use a length of twine. Set the position by tacking the twine to the frame and pulling it tightly over the upholstery to the point at which the joint is to finish. On tub chairs, for example, twine can be pulled and fixed near to each of the back legs. This will give a true, evenly curving line to which the coverings can be fitted, and later, sewn up together. Another good example of how this technique is used is on the back corners of a chesterfield sofa. The twines, which should be pulled and set very tight, are usually left on the work and covered over with the waddings and fabric. Once they are in place, the upholstery covers can be folded back and snipped towards the twine line before being fitted and cut to within 10mm (⅜in) of the twine. This leaves a seam allowance for the machine-sewn seam, which may be plain or piped.

Before removing the covers for trimming and sewing, notch or mark the fabrics with balance marks, to ensure that the parts will be aligned when they are sewn up together.

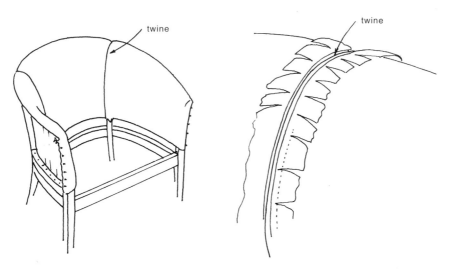

twine

twine

Twines for joint lines   Folding back and snipping the covers

LOOPS FOR LASHING

On chairs, lashings with laid cord need to have good sound fixings on the main rails. Either clout nails or 16mm (⅝in) improved tacks, which both have large heads, can be used. A laid cord has to be very stable and non-stretch, hence the fibres are laid to form the cord, with just a small amount of twist. This twist is fixed when the cord is under tension, which means that it is virtually non-stretch. This is how laid cord gets its name.

Occasionally the fixing places on frames are obstructed by arm and leg uprights, and a good fixing in line with springs is difficult. When this occurs, you can use a short loop of cord fixed to the rail each side of the obstruction, and then tie the main spring cord to this loop.

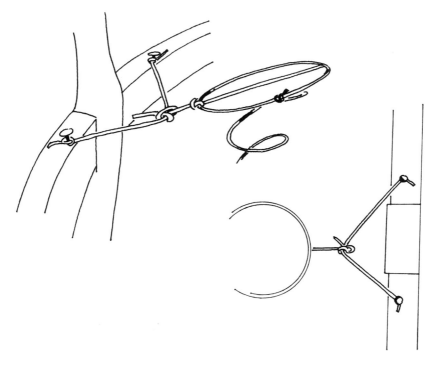

Using a loop of cord for spring lashing where
the fixing places are obstructed

Another similar problem crops up when a seat frame on a chair has been boxed-up, with the seat rails heightened by lengths of softwood nailed around the top of the seats. This is quite common on Victorian and Edwardian stuffover upholstery, being a commonly used method to reduce the need for stitched edge work. Softwood timbers generally have poor tack-holding properties and when nailed to a frame, cannot be trusted for lashing purposes. Such nailed-on extra rails are definitely not strong enough to take lashing, and if they are to remain in place when you are restoring, then alternative lashing points have to be found.

A good solution is to take the cords down below the seat rails and fix them there. If you decide on this method, the webbings will need to be arranged so that the spaces between webs are in line with the centre of the springs.

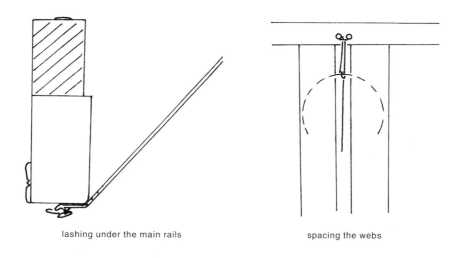

lashing under the main rails   spacing the webs

Lashing under the main rails where the seat frame has been boxed up

To improve the quality of upholstery on seats of this kind, a good 12oz (340g) quality hessian should be used over the stuffing.

LOOSE SEATS, FRENCH STYLE

It is normal in English traditional upholstery to use only two coverings on loose seats. After a good first stuffing of curled hair, the seat is shaped and pulled down in calico. An average loose seat will need 560g (1¼lb) of curled hair. The second covering is the top fabric, which is usually preceded by wadding. All the work of shaping and hard pulling is done with the calico lining. With a good foundation like this, the top cover can be applied as required, soft pull or hard, depending on the covering and its strength.

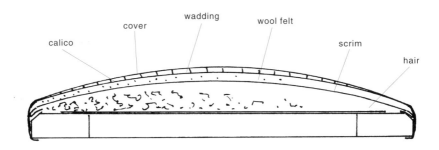

Sectional view of a loose seat, French style

A loose seat upholstered in the French style has an additional layer of scrim over the first stuffing of hair. It therefore has three covers in all, with this light second stuffing before the calico. If this method is to be used, you will need to chamfer the top outer edge of the frame. The turned-in scrim can then be fixed to this chamfered surface using fine, 6mm (¼in) tacks. This creates a very stable, well-shaped foundation.

At the corners, trim the scrim very close and turn it in, down to a tight point, with no pleating. Set the tacking close and well to the centre of the chamfer, with no overhanging tack heads.

You have a choice for the second stuffing; it can be wool, cotton felt, or a fine, soft layer of loose, curled hair. Cashmere goat hair is now becoming a

Cotton felt is used here as a soft second stuffing

more widely used filling for top stuffings and this can be considered for high-quality work of this kind. Cashmere handles well and has a slightly softer feel than hog or cow hair. Pull the second stuffing down tightly with calico and tack it to the outer edges of the frame. When the seat is the drop-in type and has to fit into a rebate, don't allow any stuffing over the frame edge.

Finally, add one thickness of good skin wadding before covering the seat.

MACHINE SEWING

For upholstery, the standard industrial, single-needle sewing machine is a lock stitch machine. A lock stitch is the most common stitch, and probably the strongest, used in machine sewing. Early machines, which were hand or treadle operated, were first produced in the middle of the nineteenth century. The first electric machines appeared in the 1920s. Since then they have developed at about the same rate as the motor car; they are now very sophisticated pieces of machinery. Today, a high-speed industrial machine can do about 5,000 stitches per minute, while a domestic machine will have a maximum speed of 1,500 stitches per minute.

Starting a seam

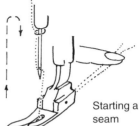

Ensure that the take-up lever is at the top of its stroke, ie, the same position as the needle bar, moving down from the top of the stroke.

Starting a seam

Needle and thread

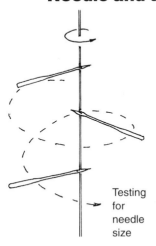

Testing for needle size

If you suspect that your needle and thread are not compatible, try this simple test; thread the needle with a short length of thread, hold the thread at both ends, vertically, to pull it taut, and twirl the needle. It should slip slowly down the thread as it spins. If it doesn't, or if it slides too quickly, you may need to change the needle for one of a different size.

Thread twist and balance

A needle thread, to sew properly, must have a left twist and the correct balance. To test the twist, hold the thread horizon-tally with your thumbs about 50mm (2in) apart, and twirl it towards you with your right thumb and index finger. If it has the

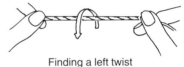

Finding a left twist

proper twist for sewing, the strands will tighten; if not, they will unwind. To test the balance, cut about 1m (1yd) of thread and hold one end in each hand. Bring the ends towards each other, so they are about 8mm (3in) apart; if the loop of thread twists about itself, the thread is unbalanced and will not perform well in a machine.

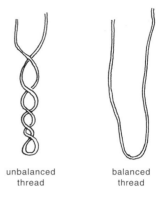

unbalanced
thread

balanced
thread

Skipped stitches on a corner

The most common cause of skipped or slipped stitches on corners is turning the fabric on the needle. This causes the loop formation, below the throat plate, to distort, which in turn, causes it to miss the pick up by the rotating hook. The result of this is that no stitch is made at the corner. To prevent this happening, put the needle down into the fabric, and bring it up by about 6mm (¼in) *before* turning the material on the needle; the loop will now be caught by the hook and the correct stitch will be formed at the corner.

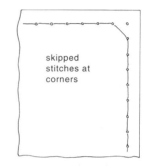

skipped
stitches at
corners

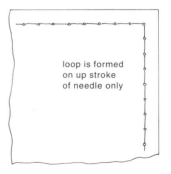

loop is formed
on up stroke
of needle only

Use the same method when the subsequent or second fabric is being sewn in, as there will now be four thicknesses or plies for the machine to cope with. Alternatively, turn the work over as the second ply is applied. This provides a clear guide for the sewing line and also places the second ply at the bottom from where it is fed in directly by the feed dog.

Try these different techniques to find which suits your own work and your own particular machine, and adjust to suit different types of cover.

NAILING

The tacking hammer used to put upholstery nails into a chair needs to have a good clean, undamaged face. You should choose the heaviest hammer that you have, so that the nails go in quickly and are not struck more than is necessary. In this way damage to the nail heads is kept to the very minimum. Fabric damage can also be a problem if the nails are hammered too tightly into the cloth or cover.

For close nailing there should be a small space, about 1mm ($\frac{1}{16}$in), between each nail. Nails should be carefully arranged at corners so that there is one placed each side of a square corner and a centre nail on a rounded corner. All the corners on a chair or stool should be treated in the same way to give a good visual balance.

 Close nailing on a braid

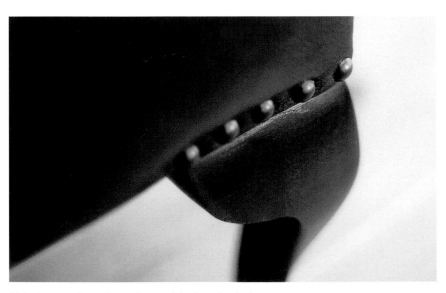

Upholstery nails positioned around the leg of a chair

When spaced nailing is the chosen option, you will need to turn the covering in to hide the raw edges, or to lay a braid or gimp along the edge before nailing. Braid and gimp are used by French upholsterers for both close and spaced nailing.

When leathers and hides are being finished with nailed edges, they can be trimmed with a very sharp knife before nailing, as they are non-fray. Alternatively, a banding can be cut from oddments of the hide. This should be cut about the width of the nail head or, to form a thicker banding, twice that width, then folded. The banding should be set in place with the cut edge down, or against show-wood.

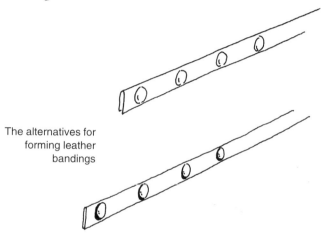

The alternatives for forming leather bandings

Fixing and spacing nails

A spiked template similar to a wide-pronged comb can be used to find the centres for close nailing, but with a little practice, your eye will be trained to judge the distance and you will find this unnecessary. Space nailing, however, is more difficult to guess and does need to be marked accurately. There are three methods commonly used to do this.

The first is to use a short rule or a stick, notched or marked with the spaces. The spacing for spaced nailing is traditionally 30mm (1¼in) centres or, if preferred, a little shorter at 25mm (1in) centres. These measurements are not carved in stone and can be varied to suit your work, they are simply historical and based on a craft tradition.

The second method is to use strong pins to mark the required centres on the edge, tapping them in with the hammer at the intervals needed.

The third method is to use gimp pins to fix the cover, braid or banding at the centres, marking the centres required with chalk. The gimp pins will then be lost under the nail heads.

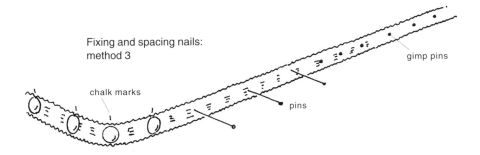

Fixing and spacing nails: method 3

chalk marks

gimp pins

pins

Some of the hardwoods used for chair making, such as oak, walnut, and various mahoganies, can be very hard. If the nails start to bend or buckle, then a sharp punch or bradawl can be used to put in a pilot hole for each nail. This will slow the nailing process down, but fewer nails will be wasted.

Beech, birch, ash, and African mahogany are less hard and will not usually give any problems when nailing.

NON-FOAM UPHOLSTERY

There has been an increase in the use of rubberized hair in recent years by both manufacturers and individuals. This is due largely to the demand by consumers who prefer, for many reasons, to have their homes free of plastic foams. Plastic foam is a fire hazard and has been the subject of legislation in

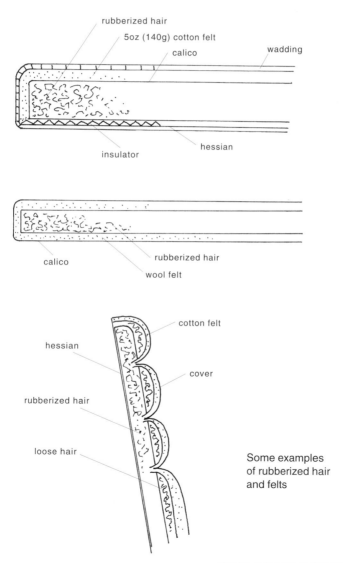

Some examples
of rubberized hair
and felts

the UK since 1988, for both commercial and domestic use. Since then it has been re-engineered and is generally much safer. However, many people prefer to avoid the faint possibility of danger and choose to buy non-foam upholstery. All upholstery materials have been affected by the foam problem and, in the UK, are now fire resistant to various standards.

Rubberized hair is a resilient filling and relatively free of synthetics and oil-based ingredients, though not entirely. A small percentage of the rubberizing compounds used are, or can be, synthetic rubbers. As a seating medium rubberized hair is limited, but for general and light use, it is very acceptable as a main filling.

A good combination for use on chair backs, arms and platforms is sheet-rubberized hair, topped with 2½ or 5oz (70 or 140g) cotton felt. This combination also works well for bed headboards, stools, pouffes, deep buttoning and window seats. The combination of rubberized hair and felt is then covered with calico and finished with a top layer of fire retardant (FR) polyester wadding. This produces a strong but comfortable type of upholstery with a traditional feel, which is foam free.

When a good cushion filling is needed to complete a piece of non-foam upholstery, the choice is usually a feather and down mixture.

PHOTOGRAPHING YOUR WORK

Fortunately, pieces of furniture do not move once they have been placed in position for taking pictures. This means that you can concentrate on the other essentials, such as composition, lighting and angles. Whenever possible, fill the frame and keep the background plain and simple. Backgrounds should be unobtrusive, being plain colours or shot out of focus so that the subject is isolated.

Cameras such as the SLR types are generally the best, at a reasonable cost, for having control over the picture and the composition. You need to be able to set the depth of field and the focus manually. You also need to be able to let the camera, once it is set up, take the picture for you. To do this, the camera should be on a tripod and should have a 10-second delay mechanism. Some compact cameras can be used in the same way, provided they are not autofocus and that the flash can be cancelled.

Lighting

For lighting I use available light, so when there is not enough natural light, I don't take pictures. If the space for photography is limited in a room or workshop, then do it outdoors but not in bright sunlight. Sunlight is very strong and creates deep shadows and too much contrast. A bright but hazy or cloudy day is ideal. North light, I am told, is the best kind for evenly lit pictures, producing pictures with good natural colour.

A large reflector is a great help in getting some reflected light onto the dark side of a subject. A reflector can be made from a piece of hardboard, either painted brilliant white or covered with some kitchen foil. The bigger the board the better, but it should be at least 750mm (30in) square. The main light source can then be reflected back onto the subject to fill darker shadow areas or to brighten the light that is already there and remove unwanted shadow. When you want to take close-up pictures, a reflector will help you to paint the subject with light, before you press the shutter.

A plain background, a reflector and a tripod all help to get good results

Lenses

A standard 50mm lens is good for general photography and usually allows you to get closer than half a metre from the subject. In addition, a small zoom lens will enable you to take wider angles and compose a picture by bringing the subject nearer. A zoom lens of 35–70mm range will give you a wide choice of picture types, and allow you to bring the picture nearer when the space is confined.

Film

By using ambient light photography and supporting a camera on a tripod, the delayed action mechanism is used all the time to get very sharp, natural looking photographs. With this method, film speed is not very important, provided the camera, either compact or SLR, has an automatic metre. This means that you don't have to worry about exposure. The camera will adjust to whichever film you put in. However, if the photos are to be enlarged, the slower films – 100 ASA or less – will give more finely grained pictures.

PILE FABRIC

If you have a pile fabric and it is not obvious which way the pile runs or is laying, then in most cases you can find the direction with a small coin. Lay out the fabric on a table surface, place a small coin on the pile, and tap the

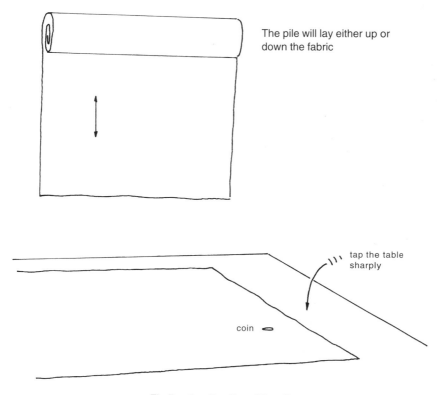

The pile will lay either up or down the fabric

tap the table sharply

coin

Finding the direction of the pile

table sharply near the coin. The vibration will cause the coin to move slowly in the direction of the lay or nap. Check this again, and then run your fingers softly up and down the fabric surface to confirm that the feel is smoother with the pile than against it. A good many velvets, velours and cut moquettes will have a very distinct lay of pile which can normally be detected by feel, with the fingers. Shading will also tell you; when light hits the surface, a

Pile fabric appears darker when you look into the direction of the pile

The same fabric appears lighter when you look across the direction of the pile

fabric with pile will appear a darker shade as you look against the pile direction, and a lighter shade as you look in the pile direction.

It is important in upholstery that you are able to determine the direction of pile on any pile surface fabric. The parts can then be correctly upholstered on a piece of work, with the pile direction running down on arms and backs, forward on seats, from back to front, and down towards the floor on all outside parts. This is the conventional treatment for pile fabrics and ensures that their wear is maximized and that visually, they are at their most attractive.

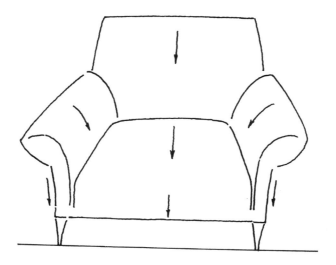

The conventional treatment for the direction of pile on a chair

PINCH QUILTING

Quilting a fabric onto a piece of ply or card is an interesting way of creating texture with plain fabrics. Small pinch-quilted panels can be made as inserts for boxes to give them soft, padded interior surfaces to hold such things as a gavel or jewellery.

First, cut a piece of stiff card or thin plywood to fit into a space, with a good allowance all round for fabric thickness, then cut the fabric at least 100mm (4in) longer and wider than the board. The pinch quilting will take up most of this extra fabric, leaving enough just to fold over the edge and glue down.

Pinch quilting creates interesting textures

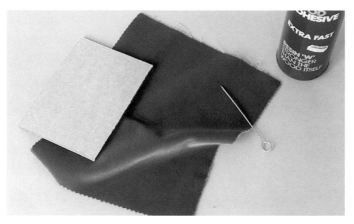

The ingredients for quilting a small panel

Begin by coating the board with plenty of glue. A heavy-duty wallpaper paste is ideal; a ready-made border paste and PVA wood glue, diluted with a little water, are also suitable. Next, apply some glue thinly to the back of the fabric – not too much or it will bleed through. Lay the fabric face down with the board placed in the centre with equal amounts around the edges.

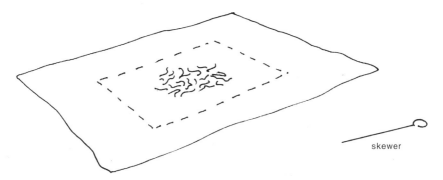

skewer

Begin quilting in the centre

Start at the middle, and begin pinching the fabric, with very small pinches, to create a rough textured surface. Use your fingers and a skewer or long needle to help move the fabric into a random pattern of tiny pinches. Turn the board occasionally to ensure that the pinches are uneven and not set in any direction. The pinched surface will gradually stiffen as the glue starts to get tacky. When the whole surface is pinched and quilted, leave it to dry.

Later, trim the fabric then fold and glue a small edge under the board, using a contact glue, to finish the panel. Finally, glue the panel into the box to hold it firmly in place.

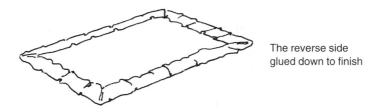

The reverse side
glued down to finish

The best fabrics for this kind of work are tightly woven and fine pile fabrics such as velours and velveteens.

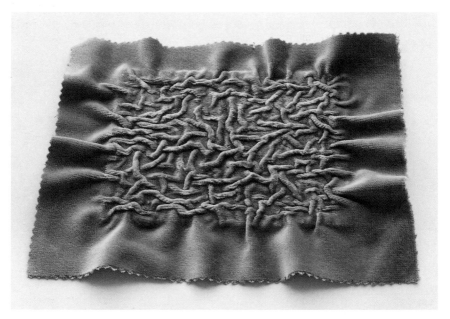

Cotton velvets produce interesting surfaces

PIPING APPLICATION

Make sure that the pressure of your piping foot is at its minimum for piping work. This helps to reduce drag as the piping is sewn onto a panel. A needle-feed machine is the ideal for upholstery sewing as it helps to get positive and equal feed on the fabric and the piping. However, if your machine is the normal drop-feed type, you can help the feed by using the manual adjustment while sewing.

Your right hand should hold the cover while your left hand guides, and pushes a little, on the piping. This technique will help reduce drag and assist the piping to feed evenly with the fabric panel. In practice, this means that the piping is slightly arched as it goes under the foot, while the main panel is kept slightly taut. Of course, you must take care not to hold back the materials and let the machine feed normally: this is a different technique which compensates for any drag produced by the foot pressure.

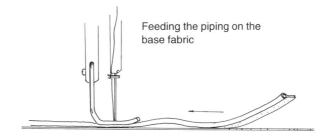

Feeding the piping on the base fabric

The piping should be slightly arched as it goes under the foot

PIPING WIDTH

Sewing seams for upholstery are always rigidly set so that everyone works to the same allowances and tolerances. The accepted allowance is 10mm (⅜in); more is cumbersome and unnecessary and less would leave them at risk of fraying, especially on some loosely woven covers. Only on leatherwork are seams reduced down further – to about 7mm (⁵⁄₁₆in) – because hides are non-fray and are more bulky than fabric plies.

It is seam allowance that governs the width at which strips of fabric should be cut for pipings. Whether they are cut straight on the fabric grain or on the bias, they are always 38mm (1½in) wide, assuming, of course, that the piping being made will have an average size cord of about 4mm (³⁄₁₆in). This width of strip, when folded over a cord and sewn, will produce a flange – the distance from the sewing line to the cut edges – of about 10mm (⅜in). The piping is then exact and will take up the same seam allowance of 10mm (⅜in) when it is machined onto the main cover.

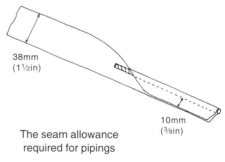

The seam allowance required for pipings

Precise cutting and exact allowances will produce a flange of about 10mm (⅜in)

PLANNING

Assuming that you have the tools, some upholstery materials and a piece of furniture to work on, restoring and re-upholstering still requires some planning. It usually pays to take a long look at what may be involved before taking a piece of upholstery apart. As soon as a chair is dismantled, it can become a confusing pile of bits and pieces. Avoid this happening; careful planning and recording of notes will make the job more enjoyable and make your aims clearer.

Take photos of the piece as you work – you never know what you will find

First, make some notes and take a photograph. Before and after pictures are always interesting and will serve to remind you of what you began with. Such pictures will eventually build a fascinating portfolio of your earlier work. Your notes should include the answers to specific questions you should ask yourself. Is the job for you or for someone else? Is there a brief?

If there isn't, should you create one? Is the existing upholstery right for the chair, or should it be altered or improved? Has the piece been previously re-upholstered, re-covered once or twice, or several times? Is it possible to tell if the upholstery is original? Is the structure or framework sound, or is it obviously shaky. Even if it seems good, be prepared to find problems when the old upholstery is removed. Are there any polished show-wood surfaces in need of attention?

You should also make more general notes about the piece, its condition overall and in detail, and the possible treatments. Can you visualize what it will look like when it is finished? Perhaps you will need to do a bit of research before you begin, if only to find a picture in a book or magazine of a similar piece. Any research will give you a more rounded view of what the work may entail and what your expectations are.

Include some measurements for the new fabric and any trimmings. With the average width of an upholstery fabric in mind – 125–140cm (49–55in) – take some generous measurements of all the cover parts on the piece, then make a rough plan on paper, fitting the parts onto a plan of the fabric. Fabric parts on a chair for example, can often be cut in pairs across the width; the two inside arms and the two outside arms can be cut as pairs, and sometimes the inside back, if not too large, can be paired with the outside back.

Parts for cushions can always be paired, and facings can and should be cut as pairs. Once you have made the rough plan, the length or vertical measurements can be totalled to give an indication of how much covering should be purchased. Trimmings, such as gimp or fringe, can usually be measured accurately, and totalled in metres to make the purchase. However, if it appears that there are unseen areas, or the design is complex, then it is best to wait until all the coverings have been removed to do a final check on sizes. The type of upholstery fabric intended for the chair will also have some bearing on the amount needed. Large patterns with long repeats will usually need more than a plain fabric.

Good evidence of earlier, and original, work

Most types of upholstered furniture can be stripped of their coverings in the reverse order to which they were applied. As the removal work proceeds and the coverings are taken off, they can be kept in a bag to be checked again later. Any shaped or tailored cover parts should certainly be kept for copying. As stripping continues, you will need to assess if some of the basic upholstery is still sound and clean enough to be retained for use again, or not removed at all. Seat areas on chairs, for example, are always the first to deteriorate, but arm and back upholstery may well be in good re-usable condition.

Restoring upholstery is a continuous problem-solving business but, viewed as a whole, and with a clear aim in mind, most projects will grow on you and be interesting and enjoyable.

PLEATING TEMPLATE

Pleated effects crop up in upholstery every so often, for valances, cabinet linings, and on worktables. Fine cottons and silks are used mainly in cabinetwork, where knife pleating is a typical Victorian treatment. Glazed or unglazed cabinet doors can have pleated silks as a lining decoration. Regency and Victorian worktables have a suspended or rigid area under the work surface, where sewing materials are stored. These areas are often covered with pleated silks.

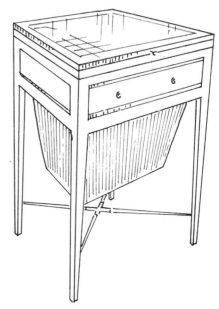

An eighteenth-century ladies' worktable – the pleated silkwork bag hangs below

Prepare the brown paper pattern

In keeping with original styles, the fabrics used are usually fine and nearly always pleated. The treatments are usually knife pleats, with about 13mm (½in) spacing. Making a template or pattern to create your pleating keeps the work consistent and speeds up what can be a fiddly business. Make the pattern from a strong brown paper to any manageable size, drawing pencil lines to mark the size of the pleats required. Alternative spaces should be double the pleat width, to allow for folding. To complete the pattern, fold it from one line to the next in a knife-pleat formation. Make the folds in the paper permanent with an electric iron.

Then make the folds permanent with a hot iron

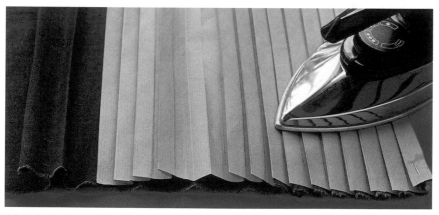

After pinning, press the pleats one at a time

A knife-pleated sample

The pattern is now ready to use on any fine fabric. A table with a clean, smooth surface is essential, along with a long, flat metal straightedge: this can be used as a weight and to assist with the folding. Lay the fabric out flat, face up, with the pattern over the top. Pin the leading edge of the fabric and the pattern together and begin folding and ironing each pleat, one at a time, using the metal straightedge to ease the fabric into the pattern folds. The brown paper protects the fabric as each pleat is ironed and pressed sharp.

The completed fabric panel can be left with a weight on it to keep it flat until needed, or temporarily tacked to a frame for checking.

REMOVING CANEWORK

Prewoven sheet canework, as with traditional canework, is vulnerable when it becomes old or is misused. It is mostly in seats that the cane will fracture, and this is impossible to repair or patch – the whole of the seat has to be removed and replaced with a freshly woven cane panel.

Because a cane seat is glued into a deep groove in the framework, removing the old cane is the most time-consuming part of the job. Once the old cane has been removed, and the groove cleaned out and made ready, putting the new piece in is relatively easy.

The secret to removing the old, damaged panel is to have the right tools. A narrow, 4 or 5mm (⅛ or ³⁄₁₆in) mortise chisel or bevel-edge chisel is ideal; alternatively, a screwdriver of the same size sharpened to a chisel point will do. Also necessary is a piece of 5mm (³⁄₁₆in) steel rod or a good nail punch, to clean out the glue and bits of old cane from the deep groove. Either should have a good clean, flat face so that the glue is sheared from the bottom and the walls of the groove. Some fairly coarse sandpaper and an electric drill with a 4 or 5mm (⅛ or ³⁄₁₆in) drill bit will help to clean out and smooth the groove. Finally, a lightweight wooden mallet is needed to tap the chisel or the screwdriver, and to work the nail punch slowly along the groove.

The other tools required are those used to prepare and fix the new canework. A staple gun is essential, either spring loaded, electric or pneumatic. Whichever type is to hand, it must have a nose which is no more than 5mm (³⁄₁₆in) thick and this nose should protrude from the gun so that staples can be fired deep into the bottom of the groove with plenty of pressure. A pair of trimming scissors is needed to trim the new cane panel to size and a sharp knife is also necessary. To complete the tool list, a hammer, preferably a Warrington, is needed to tap down the narrow cane-finishing bead into the groove, after the new canework is in place.

Begin the work by carefully lifting the old 5mm (³⁄₁₆in) cane beading. Give it a good sharp tap with a chisel to dig it out. The strip may lift easily in parts but will most likely shatter and break up as it is levered out. Take care not to drift the chisel into the polished or painted surround.

Once the beading is out, the remaining canework can also be removed; if necessary, help this along with a knife. Now use the rod or punch to dig out the remaining debris – it is likely that the original canework will not have been stapled in. Use the drill for the final cleaning by running it carefully along the groove, drawing it slowly towards you. Sandpaper the edges to complete the cleaning out.

The broken cane seat removed in one piece

REPLACING CANEWORK ON MODERN CHAIRS

Most craft shops and some DIY stores will stock the standard design of woven cane sheet, which is made in widths of about 50 or 60cm. A ½m length will usually be enough for a single chair seat. A length of 5mm (³⁄₁₆in) diameter cane beading, long enough to go round the whole seat, can be bought at the same time. PVA wood glue works well for this job; although it is not a gap-filling glue, it runs well into the groove, and as it is water based, it can be easily cleaned off with a wet cloth or tissue.

Cut the new canework panel to fit the seat, with enough over to go down into the groove, plus a few millimetres. Use some newspaper, or a piece of calico or polythene, and a felt-tip pen to make an accurate pattern. Check this pattern for fit by pushing all the outer edges down into the groove, and trim as necessary. Cut the canework panel to the pattern. Next, in a large sink, a bath or a shower basin, immerse the panel completely in cold water. You will need to weight it down and keep it flat under water for about 45 minutes. While this is soaking, push the beading lightly into the groove and cut it exactly to length. The beading should not be soaked in water.

After about 40 minutes, run some glue into the groove and spread it with an odd piece of the beading so that glue is coating the sides of the groove. Shake off the excess water from the cane panel and lay it on the seat, making sure that the weave is straight and square. Ease the centre back edge down into the groove with a regulator, and fire two or three staples to hold it. Stretch the panel lightly to the centre front of the seat and do the same. Repeat this process for the two centre sides. The remaining edges can now be pushed down into place and the stapling continued. Clean the nozzle of the gun with a wet rag if necessary. You may need to trim the cane edges here and there, if there are any edges protruding up from the groove.

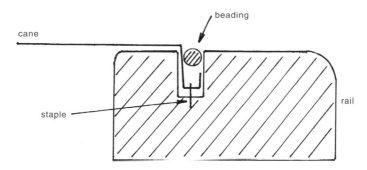

cane

beading

rail

staple

The groove and canework set in a modern chair seat

Because of the nature of the glue, and the fact that the cane is wet, there is plenty of time to fix the cane well into the groove and ensure that the panel will automatically tighten as it dries out. When you are happy with the first fixing, run some more glue – not too much – into the groove and begin gently tapping the bead down. It should be a tight fit and will need tapping down with a hammer, but should not go down below the level of the timber edge. Excess glue will ooze from the groove; wipe this away with a wet cloth so that the bead is clean and free of glue.

Leave the chair to dry out slowly at room temperature; it will need at least eight hours. As it dries, the new canework will become very tight; it is best left unused for about 24 hours.

The new woven canework finished with a beading

RUCHING BORDERS

Ruching is the term used in upholstery to describe gathering. A ruched border on a piece of upholstery adds interest by creating a textured surface and can be very attractive.

A border strip should be ruched by hand, ready for stitching in place on a chair or stool. The three methods used are all basically the same; it is a matter of preference as to which you adopt.

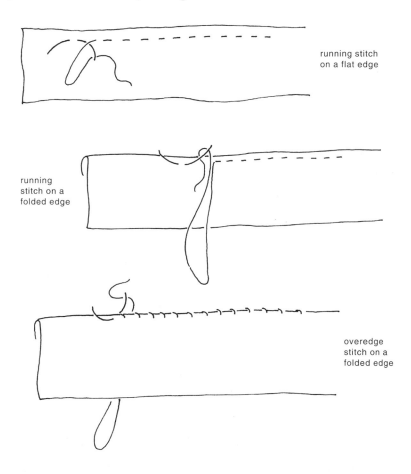

running stitch on a flat edge

running stitch on a folded edge

overedge stitch on a folded edge

Alternative methods for ruching a border

Two of the methods involve putting in a running stitch with a strong thread and the other, putting in overedge stitching along the top of a folded edge. The options are to:

- put in a close running stitch about 10mm (⅜in) from the fabric edge;
- fold and turn the edge of the fabric over about 10mm (⅜in), and put in a running stitch close to the folded edge;
- fold down the edge about 10mm (⅜in) and sew an overedge stitch along the folded edge.

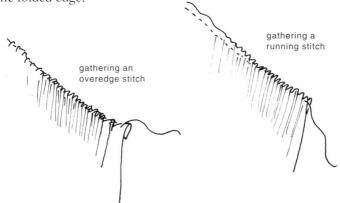

gathering a
running stitch

gathering an
overedge stitch

Gathering the fabric for a ruched border

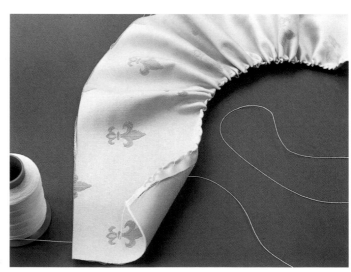

An overedge
stitch produces
a neat, well
formed gather

When pulled up and gathered, ready for applying, a ruched strip can be reduced by about 50%, though this is variable. Pin the border in place on or under the edge, then pad it with wadding and ruche in the bottom edge with tacks to complete it. The top edge of the border can then be slip stitched and corded to conceal the edge joint.

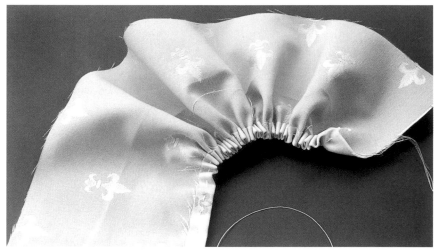

A running stitch can be used to draw up a folded edge

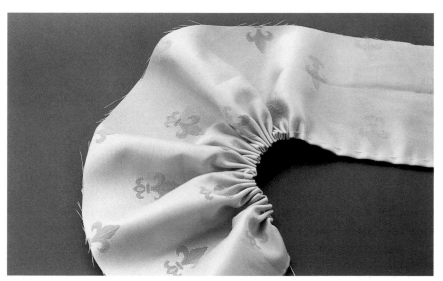

The face side of a prepared border

SELLING IN CALICO

If you are doing some traditional upholstery and want to either sell the piece privately or put it on display for auction, it is sometimes better to do it up to calico and then find a customer before finishing it, rather than buying a covering and finishing it first: everyone's taste is different, so selling in calico is less risky and can save money.

Presentation, when selling, is all-important and can make the difference between a quick sale and a slow one. Here are two ways of smartening up a chair in calico. Buy some plain, inexpensive braid in a cream colour and use this to trim the edges and hide the tacking. This will tidy up the piece and make it look almost finished and a little more attractive. The braid can be fixed on with white gimp pins or with a few spots of glue so that removal later is no problem.

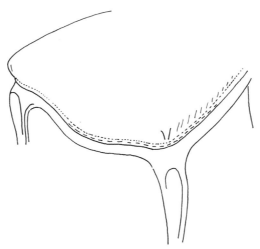

A temporary braid to hide the tacking

Another way of making calico look temporarily more attractive is to run a fancy stitch around the main edges of the chair. Choose a bright colour thread, which will take the eye away from the raw edges of the calico, and use a small slipping needle to put in a large, double zigzag stitch and embroider the main edges of the piece. The zigzag stitches will give a chain-like effect around the calico. Removing the lightly caught stitch later is very quick, and if the chair is to be padded with wadding before covering, then it need not be removed at all.

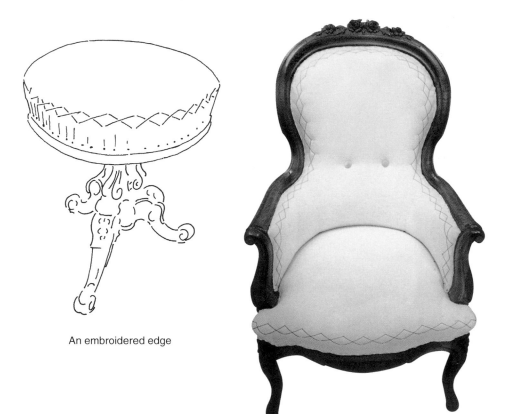

An embroidered edge

A small Victorian armchair in calico, embroidered around the main edges

SHOW-WOOD EDGES

Art Deco furniture designs incorporated veneered panels and show-wood surrounds in different finishes and timbers. Chairs and settees were no exception, with veneered plywoods used for facings and the outer surfaces of arms and backs.

Close nailing and plain braids were used extensively to finish upholstery along polished or painted timber edges. The following interesting technique was developed to use when a plain or piped edge was preferred. Fix a piping or folded strip of fabric along the outer line of a chair arm or back, set into a rebate and against the show-wood, with small tacks or staples. Make this very firm with a fibre or card tacking strip set tightly against the cover strip or piping, apply a cotton wadding, then pin and slip stitch the upholstery fabric to this. The tacking strip secures the edge and holds it firmly against the show-wood. This produces upholstery that appears panelled and plain in its finish, without the need for nailing or braids. Visually, this suited Art Deco designs, but the technique can be applied to any traditional upholstery where a fabric has to be finished to a show-wood edge.

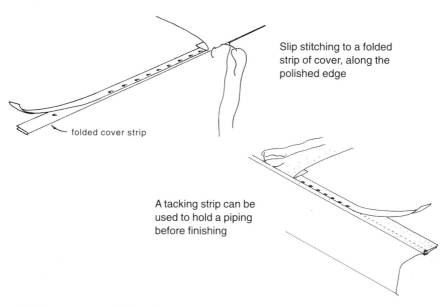

Slip stitching to a folded strip of cover, along the polished edge

folded cover strip

A tacking strip can be used to hold a piping before finishing

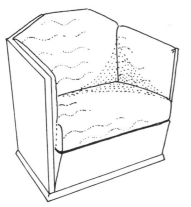

A typical
Art Deco
chair design

A cotton wadding
is applied before
the covering

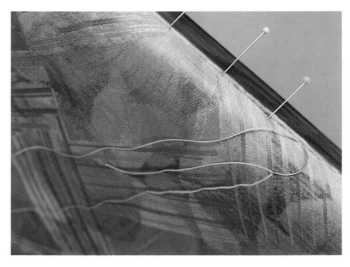

The cover is
pinned and
slip stitched
to the piping

SLIP STITCHING

The 3in (75mm) circular slipping needle is a good size for general hand-stitch work. Ideal for most upholstery covers, it has the right amount of curve for dealing with fixed traditional upholstery. One size smaller is the 2½in (63mm) needle. This is not only shorter but has a finer gauge, and is perfect for fine, close stitching of fabrics such as silks and cottons, or when a closer slip stitch is needed.

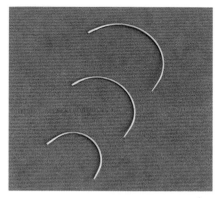

Three sizes of curved slipping needle: 3, 2½ and 2in (75, 63 and 50mm)

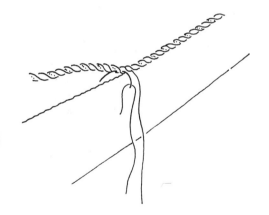

Using a cording needle

The 2½in (63mm) needle is often referred to as a cording needle because its sharper curve and finer gauge make it ideal for sewing upholstery cords into edges and facings. A cord trimming demands tight, close stitches to hold it firmly in place. A slipping thread can be used for this or, if preferred, a strong, corespun machine thread, run through some beeswax; this will pass through a cord more easily and give good results.

The size of a curved needle is measured along the curve of the needle and not across from eye to point. Very small 2in (50mm) needles are available, but only very small fingers will be able to handle such fine tools.

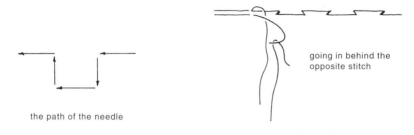

going in behind the
opposite stitch

the path of the needle

Working a slip stitch

The slip stitch is still the most useful of all the stitches used in upholstery for closing and finishing fabrics and covers. For best results, use stitches about 7mm (⁵⁄₁₆in) long and each time you enter the cloth, go in just before where the opposite stitch came out. Repeat this along the seam with every stitch and pull tight every three or four stitches to align and close the joint. A matching thread will not be seen using this technique.

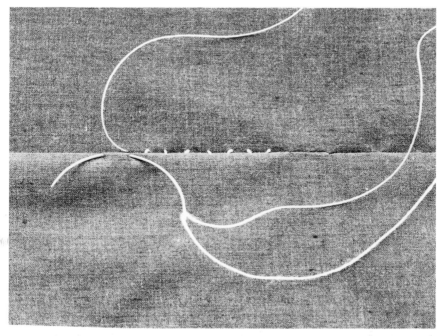

A white slipping thread has been used here to show the pattern of a slipping stitch

Closing hides and vinyl fabrics with slip stitching is very difficult, if not impossible, because of the nature of these materials. However, if necessary, and if you want to close either of these by hand, machine a strip of soft fabric along each of the two edges to be closed; these can then be slipped very closely together along the machined seam.

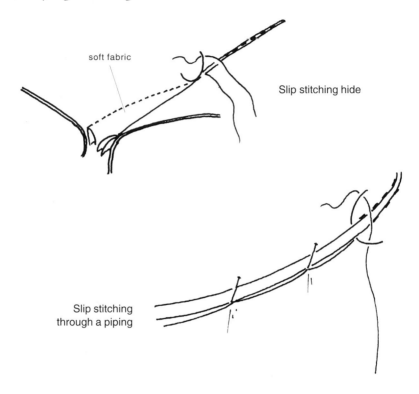

soft fabric

Slip stitching hide

Slip stitching through a piping

SPRING WIRE GAUGES

Choose 10swg double-cone springs as the norm for 4, 5 and 6in (100, 125 and 150mm) sizes in seats. This produces comfortably supported seating when the springs are in groups of five or more. Nine springs, as an example, will fit nicely into an average size chair seat or eight for a tub chair with a 'D' shaped seat.

Beware of the hard seat, which for most people is too firm to be comfortable. The 9swg hourglass spring should be used with caution on fixed traditional seats, except for deep springing. However, $9\frac{1}{2}$ and 9swg springs can be considered at the above heights when a spring seat is to be a platform for a foam- or feather-filled cushion. Upholstery, after all, should be comfortable and not necessarily built to last 50 years.

The same principle can be adopted for the springing of chair backs. Use 12, 14 and 16swg springs and make them comfortable and welcoming. Lighter gauges but more springs is a good formula for comfort.

Imperial standard wire gauge sizes

Standard wire gauge	Inches	Nearest fraction of an inch		Nearest metric gauge
7	0.176	$\frac{3}{16}$	0.187	4.5
8	0.160	$\frac{5}{32}$	0.156	4.0
9	0.144			3.6
10	0.128	$\frac{1}{8}$	0.125	3.3
11	0.116			3.0
12	0.104			2.7
13	0.092	$\frac{3}{32}$	0.093	2.4
14	0.080			2.1
15	0.072			1.9
16	0.064	$\frac{1}{16}$	0.062	1.65
17	0.056			1.45
18	0.048			1.25
19	0.040			1.05
20	0.036			0.95
21	0.032			0.85
22	0.028	$\frac{1}{32}$	0.031	0.72

A standard wire gauge showing 37 different gauges or thicknesses

Selecting springs

	Gauge (swg)	Height	Type
Seats	8½	8–9in (200–225mm)	d/cone or hourglass
	9	6–7in (150–175mm)	ditto
	10	5–6in (125–150mm)	ditto
Arms	11	5in (125mm)	ditto
	12	4–5in (100–125mm)	ditto
Backs	12	6in (150mm)	ditto
	14	5–6in (125–150mm)	ditto
	16	4–5in (100–125mm)	ditto

STIFF CARD LININGS

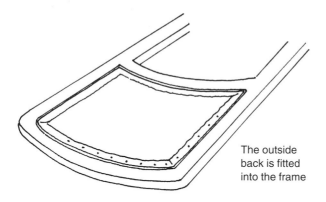

The outside back is fitted into the frame

Lining an outside back on a chair with stiff card gives a smooth, attractive finish. Normally, outside backs are supported with hessian and waddings, which is fine for most stuffover work. A card lining is used on traditional work only when an outside back cover goes into a chair and the subsequent upholstery is built onto it. This happens with pinstuffed backs and curved panel chair backs, such as French-style show-wood and bergére chairs.

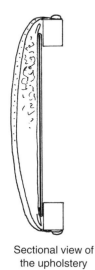

Sectional view of the upholstery

The technique is also useful when fine silk or cotton fabrics are used as coverings. The card support will completely disguise the pressure exerted by the upholstery on a delicate fabric and reduce the possibility of tack bites appearing when a fine fabric is stretched and fixed into a frame.

Prepare the card to fit into the frame with enough allowance for an adequate fixing with tacks or staples. Bend the card into place and mark it accurately, then trim to size. Fit and spot glue the edges of the cover to the inside of the card, making allowances for stretch on shaped work. As it is glued with a quick-setting contact adhesive, the cover should only be stretched a little, so that there is no possibility of distorting the card or unnecessarily distorting the fabric.

Try the panel in place, check for any wrinkles, and check that the fabric grain is taut and the vertical and horizontal lines are good. When all of these are fine, the panel is ready for fixing in place before the inside back upholstery continues.

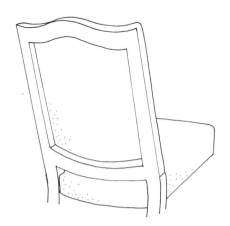

A good finish is produced with card and cover

A French chair with the outside back and stiff card fitted

STITCHWORK: STARTING AND STOPPING

The upholsterers' knot is a slipknot, which is used to begin most types of thread or twine work. It can be a single or a double knot; both are formed in the same way, but a double slipknot has the benefit of a tighter grip. A slipknot is also used for holding buttons and tufts down. They can be slackened or tightened as required, before they are made permanent.

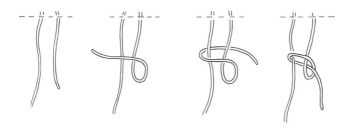

The upholsterers' knot

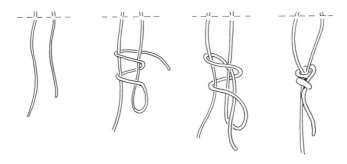

The double slipknot

If you are working a line of stitching and the twine runs out, leave a short, loose end. Start the new twine off with a slipknot, but before drawing it tight, wind the loose end into the slipknot twice, then pull it tight and trim.

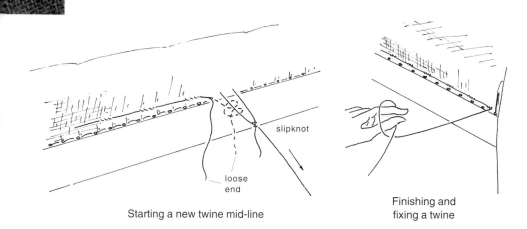

slipknot

loose
end

Starting a new twine mid-line

Finishing and
fixing a twine

At the end of a line of stitching, seal the twine tightly by making a very small second return with the needle and winding the twine clockwise to form a knot, before snipping off.

An alternative finish can be made by winding the twine around your thumb and forefinger, then grabbing the twine close up to the work and letting the knot slide and tighten up to the work. Tie again with a hitch or double hitch to finish, before trimming all the loose ends and loops off.

Wind the twine around your thumb and forefinger to form a loose knot . . .

... slide the knot up to the scrim ...

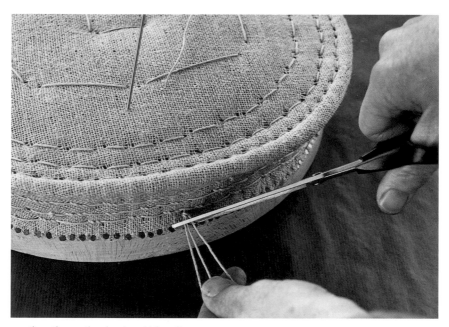

... then tie another knot and trim off

STUFFING A HAIR-FILLED SQUAB

A squab or pad for a piece of period upholstery is very similar to a miniature mattress and made in the same way. One of the problems in making up a squab lies in filling the case to a good firm density. The height or thickness of the squab is set by the borders, and the case has to be tightly filled to that level. If the stuffing height is not controlled then the case will balloon.

One way of controlling the height is to place the flat of one hand on top of the case while using your other hand to push the filling into the far end of the case – this can be tiring and time-consuming.

Jig board and stop

Using a small jig, consisting of a board and a stop, is a less tiring way to help control the filling height and to get it even and tight. Another small tool that will help to get the filling well packed is a ram. This can be made from a piece of timber 152 x 51 x 25mm (6 x 2 x 1in), with a short handle fitted to it in the form of a hammer. A ram will help in the pushing and packing once filling is under way.

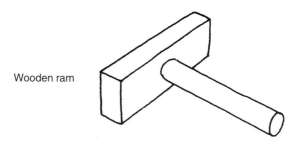

Wooden ram

The traditional stuffing stick is another very effective tool. This can be made from a 600mm (24in) length of timber, shaped with a curve and a groove at one end and cut to a two-pronged fork at the opposite end.

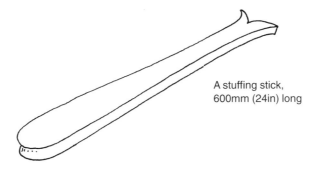

A stuffing stick, 600mm (24in) long

Use your free hand to hold the jig over the case while you proceed with the filling and ramming. Remove the jig periodically so that you can check and feel the case for tightness, even filling and density. Before you pin up the case for closing, push the last few handfuls of stuffing in with your fingers to complete the filling.

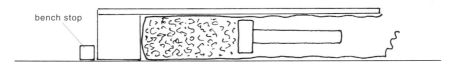

bench stop

Filling the squab

STUFFING WIRES

A stuffing wire is sometimes used in place of a stuffing rail in chairs and settees. The height of the upholstery seat is set by the upholsterer and the wire is fixed at that level. The back upholstery is then brought down to the wire to produce the tuckaway line. Leaving the fitting of the wire to the upholsterer, rather than having a fixed tacking rail or stuffing rail put in by the chair maker, leaves some flexibility in the outcome of the upholstery.

This method of setting the tuckaway line on a chair can be very useful and will allow upholstery to be adapted and redesigned. A seat with fixed upholstery, for example, can be adapted to a cushion seat with a platform by lowering the back and arm line where it meets the seat.

This technique is very common in France and you will find wires used in this way in many French chairs. Increasingly, antique chairs are finding their way into the UK from France. The sequence of working that we are used to in the UK is very often reversed by French upholsterers, so that the seat of a chair is put in first. The back and seat line is then created with a wire, which is fixed to the frame with wire staples and loops of webbing. Arm and back upholstery then follow to complete the sitting area in a chair.

Fixed wires can also be used in the centre of the backs of chairs, where a pull-in design is required. This provides a firm, curved line in the middle of a back to which hessians, calicos and covers can be fixed and stitched.

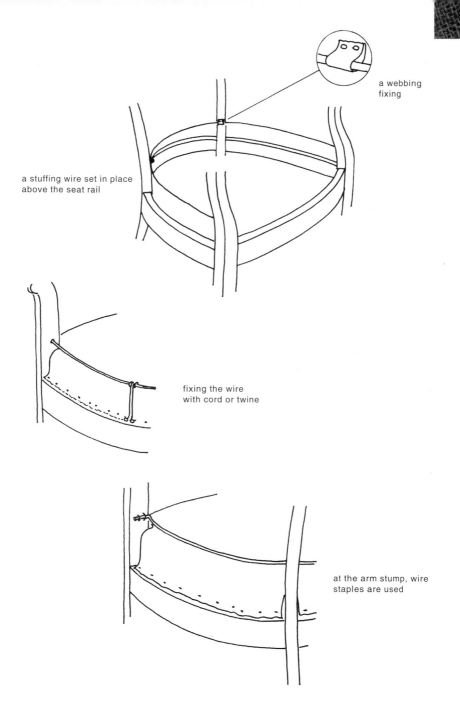

a webbing fixing

a stuffing wire set in place above the seat rail

fixing the wire with cord or twine

at the arm stump, wire staples are used

Using a stuffing wire in place of a rail

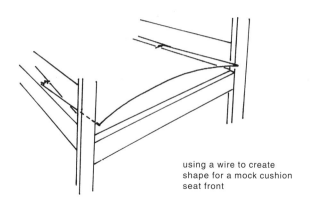

using a wire to create
shape for a mock cushion
seat front

side view:
pivoting the wire
on the seat rails

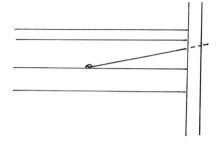

A wire set onto back rails for pull-in upholstery

Additional uses for wire in upholstery

TACK STITCHING

This is an early upholstery stitching technique which can be found on some late eighteenth-century and early nineteenth-century chairs and back stools. Although found mostly on the upholstered edges of chair backs rather than on seats, I like to think that we should continue to use very old stitching techniques, such as the tack stitch. They are effective in the way that they draw up and support stuffed-edge lines, and are basically more simple to work than some of the Victorian stitchwork that we use so much today.

The tack stitch works well to firm and support new edge rolls, for example, on chaise longue backs and small well seats. The process begins with a first stuffing, usually of hair or fibre, pulled down with scrim and tacked along a chamfered rail or flat on the outer face of the rail. When tacking down the scrim, leave a tack every 40mm (1½in) temporary, and hammer all the others in.

Use fine twine and a two-point needle, and to start the stitch off, wind the twine round the first tack and hammer it in. Push the needle into the scrim, at an angle of about 45°, and make a blind stitch by returning the needle out of the scrim at the next temporary tack. Now pull on the twine to draw out

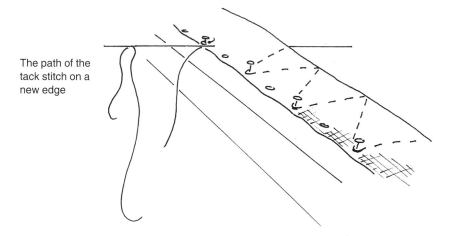

The path of the tack stitch on a new edge

the stuffing and firm the edge, then take the twine around the temporary
tack before hammering it home to hold the stitch tight. Repeat this process
by entering the scrim alongside the tack, then going on to make the blind
stitch. Because this stitch has no knots it depends on the tacks to hold the
stuffing to the edge.

Tack stitching is also used as a holding stitch when a seat or back pad from an
old chair is being re-used and put under new scrim. Original stitched pads, if
still in good shape, are often re-used in the restoration of period work. When
re-used over a new webbed base and with a new, good quality scrim, an old
stitched edge pad will preserve a small piece of our heritage. At the same
time, the original shape and outline of the upholstery is retained. To
complete the restoration, restitch the top stitching along the same line as the
old, and put in some new stuffing ties to stabilize the pad before replacing or
renewing the top stuffing.

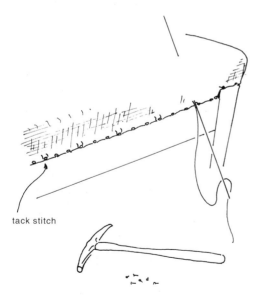

In original eighteenth-century
examples, the scrim was turned
in and tacked on the face of the
rail and not onto a chamfered
edge. The tack stitch was then
made by putting the spaced
temporary tacks above the
scrim tacks.

tack stitch

Using the tack stitch to
restore an old seat pad

TACKS AND STAPLES

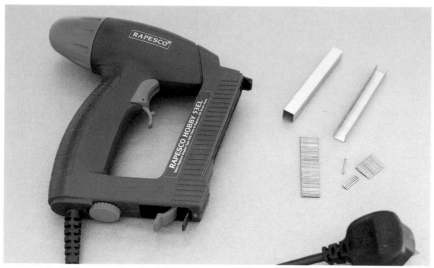

An electric staple gun with adjustable power, which fires 10 and 12mm (⅜ and ½in) staples and fine 16mm (⅝in) nails

In the mid-1950s there was a revolution waiting to happen in the upholstering industry. It was in the way that upholstery materials were being fixed to chair frames. Those manufacturers in Europe who kept a close eye on developments in the USA began to realize that the tack was going to be replaced by a quicker, cleaner, and more efficient fixing method – the staple gun, powered by compressed air and firing fine wire staples, was slowly introduced as an alternative to the hammer. Once accepted by the trade and the trade union, the new systems were adopted very quickly and, as if overnight, the fixing revolution in upholstery had changed the way we worked.

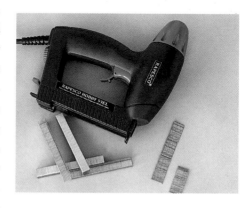

An electric staple gun for home use; lightweight and powerful, it fires staples and nails

Many other industries adopted the same new systems. For the manufacturing furniture industry, the tack was gone forever, but in the world of upholstery restoration and reupholstery, the tack is still alive and well.

The two different fixing methods live happily alongside each other, both having their advantages and disadvantages. Tack sizes range from 1in (25mm) fine down to ¼in (6mm) fine and ⅝in (16mm) improved down to ¼in (7mm) improved. Upholstery staples range in size from ⅝in (16mm) down to ⅛in (3mm), with wide and narrow crown widths.

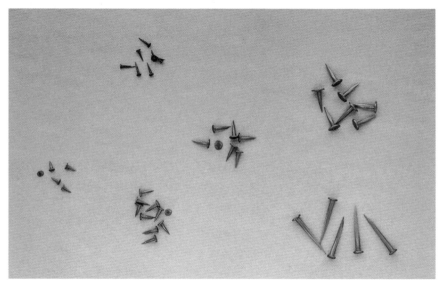

A range of blued steel upholstery tacks and gimp pins: black pins at top, 10mm (⅜in) gimp pins; left to right, 6mm (¼in) fine, 10mm (⅜in) fine, 13mm (½in) fine, 16mm (⅝in) improved and 25mm (1in) fine

The tacking hammer has changed very little in design since the 1950s while the new ranges of upholstery staple gun are always developing. Lightweight, fast and very efficient, many are now dual function and will fire fine nails as well as the wire staple.

TEAR RESISTANCE IN LEATHER

Cuts in upholstery hide, unlike in a woven fabric, are non-fray, very clean, and need to be precise. However, the tear resistance can vary in a hide, depending on its quality and the way it is applied. The thickness of hide for upholstery can also vary from 1.5mm up to 4mm (¹⁄₁₆ to ⅛in). For general upholstery purposes 1.5mm (¹⁄₁₆in) is the norm, and this will suit most conventional applications.

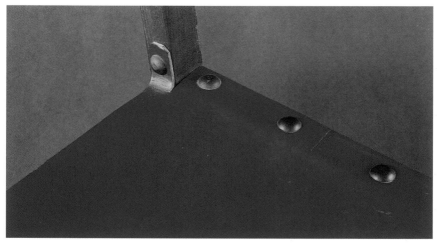

A dining chair seat using a heavy leather fixed with large brass nails

Some of the very early attempts at basic soft seating, in the seventeenth century and earlier, used thick, natural, unsplit hides. These needed to be heavy and strong. They supported the sitter, provided some flexibility, and gradually moulded themselves with use. Early attempts at webbing formations were produced from cut strips of natural hide – probably ox, cow or buffalo hide – woven together as we would arrange webbings.

Leather is an interesting seating medium and has fascinated furniture designers and upholsterers since its early use as semi-flexible seating. Some of the classic designs of the twentieth century, which continue to be reproduced, have used strong hides in different forms.

Tear test a piece of hide

You can test the tear resistance of a hide by cutting into the centre of a small sample, then trying to make it tear by straining the cut open. This is a very severe test and does not necessarily mean that the hide is poor if the resistance is low.

The tip of a cut in a piece of hide can be reinforced and made less vulnerable to tear, by simply punching a small hole. The hole should be about 6mm (¼in) in diameter and cut cleanly with an upholsterers' hole punch. In very thick hides, the hole can be a little larger. This will effectively stop tear by spreading the resistance over a larger area of the skin.

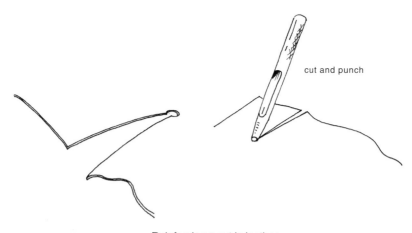

cut and punch

Reinforcing a cut in leather

TEMPLATES AND PATTERNS

For most shaped work, when curves are involved, a template is desirable. It helps to confirm that a cushion or a facing, for example, will fit well into the space provided. It can be trimmed carefully to shape, turned over, or folded at the centre and will enable you to transfer a true shape onto a lining or covering fabric. Except when repetition is likely, a part that has only straight lines can be easily measured and drawn, without the need for a template.

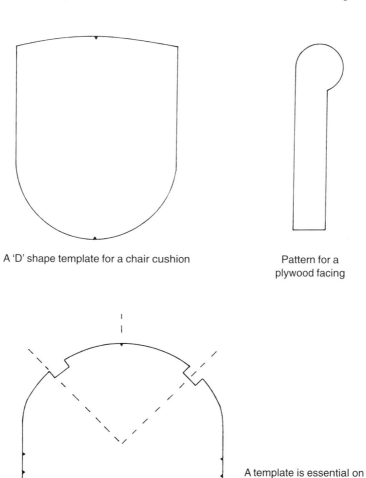

A 'D' shape template for a chair cushion

Pattern for a
plywood facing

A template is essential on
antique chairs that are no
longer symmetrical

Thick grade polythene sheeting is the perfect material for pattern and template making. Being flexible and transparent, it makes transferring the shape onto a cover easier and very accurate, especially when a design on a cover has to be matched and lined up. Another advantage is that polythene will cut to a very sharp, well-defined edge, which is perfect for drawing round. It can also be punched very precisely with a hole punch, for buttoning patterns, etc. Also important is the fact that polythene is generally very hard-wearing and does not tear easily.

Other, less permanent materials that can be used are stiff paper, calico and polypropylene linings.

See-through materials are ideal for marking out templates

THUMB ROLLS

A thumb roll is a small version of a dug roll, which is used along frame edges to insulate and soften them, and to provide a foundation for the upholstery. No doubt edges of this kind developed from the very early attempts at stuffover upholstery.

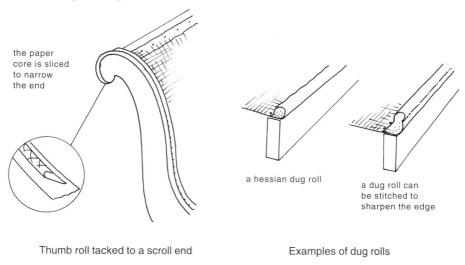

the paper core is sliced to narrow the end

a hessian dug roll

a dug roll can be stitched to sharpen the edge

Thumb roll tacked to a scroll end

Examples of dug rolls

The edge roll has a long history in upholstery and is not, as we tend to think, a quicker, cheaper alternative to the nineteenth-century stitched edge.

The eighteenth-century procedure for upholstering a chair, described in Diderot's *Encyclopedie* of 1757, included edge rolls along the front of seats. These were included in order to prevent the stuffings from collapsing under the strain of use. The extra roll was filled with hair or tow (horse hair or flax fibre) sewn into canvas, and fixed to the front rail of seats. The subsequent stuffings were then put in over the roll before being covered in linen cloth.

Today we use the roll on a frame edge for exactly the same reason. For stuffings we use coconut fibre, cotton felts or pre-formed rolls made from recycled paper. A thumb roll can be made using a strip of jute webbing

An edge roll of shredded vegetable fibre taken from a Regency chair seat

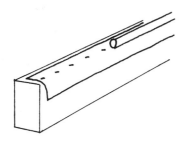

Setting the webbing
on the rail edge

An excellent thumb roll can be made using a large size, 10mm (⅜in) paper piping cord as the filling. This will sit firmly on any timber edge and works well on curves and on scroll shapes.

tacked close to the frame edge. Roll the chosen filling tightly into the centre of the web and tack the edge again to form a small, neat roll that overhangs the very edge of the rail. The thickness of the roll is controlled by the webbing width, and by using a 50mm (2in) web, which is a strong, heavy-weave material, the roll remains small.

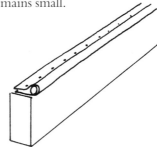

Making a thumb roll with
a large piping cord

TOOLBOX EXTRAS

Empty out an upholsterer's toolbox and the huge number of different small tools can be quite amazing. All have their various important uses, each one vital to particular aspects of the work. In addition to the obvious, the items below are worth special mention.

A box of sticky plasters to cover small wounds quickly can also be used as protection when fingers get sore.

Keeping a stick of white chalk in your toolbox is a good way of keeping it free of moisture: the chalk will absorb any dampness present, and thus help to protect the tools against corrosion. Replace the chalk with a fresh stick every so often.

The contents of an upholstery toolbox

A short length of 10mm or 13mm (⅜ or ½in) dowel has many uses. Often referred to as a 'dolly stick', such dowel, sharpened to a pencil point at one end and a smooth chisel point at the other, is used as a tool to fold and tuck fabrics and leathers.

Essential items in the toolbox

Small earplugs kept in a plastic bag can be worn when the work gets particularly noisy, as with consistent hammering.

A nail punch is very useful when the tack hammer is unable to reach into a deep corner, or when it is risky to use one, as when working near to polished edges.

A short strip of emery cloth glued to a flat length of timber is perfect for removing burrs from your needles and regulators. On the reverse side glue a strip of hide, suede side uppermost. Use this, with a stropping action, to hone and finish a point or a cutting edge to a fine sharpness.

Use PVA wood adhesive to glue the emery cloth and the suede

TOP STUFFINGS ON SQUABS

When a newly-made squab has been tufted and stitched to the required shape, it is ready for the top or outer stuffing, prior to the calico or final covering. The surface of the tufted scrim will be uneven, due to the depth of the tufting. Fill each of the indents with a small amount of loose hair to level the surface before adding a layer of cotton or wool felt; if this layer is not added, the surface will still feel uneven.

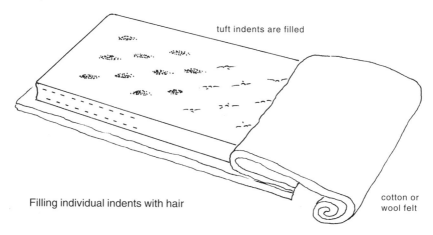

tuft indents are filled

cotton or wool felt

Filling individual indents with hair

Alternatively, lightly cover the whole surface area, on both sides of the squab, with a very thin layer of hair, then cover each side in calico, slip stitching it to the outer edges, before adding the wadding. The first method is much quicker, and leaves the squab ready to be put into a made-up cover.

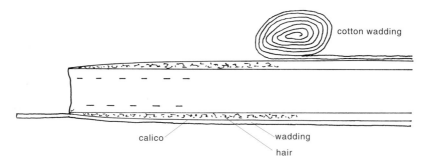

cotton wadding

calico

wadding

hair

Covering the whole surface with hair

TUFTS

Making a set of tufts for a small piece of work can be very rewarding and will add an extra dimension to your work. Handmade tufts of wool or silk were quite common in upholstery during the eighteenth century when they were used then to hold stuffings in place, though not in large numbers as you

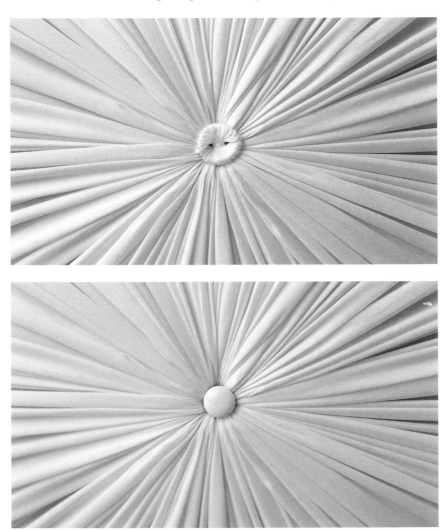

Compare the effect of the tuft with that of the button

would expect to see in later nineteenth-century furnishing. Deep buttoning had not developed as a decoration or a skill and the tufts were used quite sparingly – about five to a chair back or seat cushion.

Embroidery threads are ideal for making small button-size tufts. A length of about 1.5m (5ft) will make a good, closely wound tuft. Make yourself a tufting stick from a short length of timber. The prongs should be 3mm (¼in) thick, and measure 22mm (⅞in) across with a 4mm (³⁄₁₆in) slot cut down the middle. Sand the timber well, down to a smooth finish.

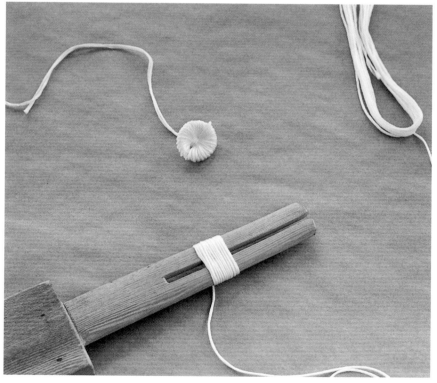

Winding the thread around the tufting stick

To make a tuft, wind the thread 16 times round the stick from left to right then overwind, back to where you started, about 12 times. Now cut the loose end off and use it to tie the centre of the tuft with three cross winds through the gap in the prongs. Tie a single knot at the back and ease the tuft off the stick, holding it firmly between your thumb and clenched fingers. Tighten the three winds a little, then lay the tuft face down, pull the centre winds very tight, and tie again. This should form the tuft into an almost circular floret. Embroidery thread can be bought in small skeins in almost every colour possible.

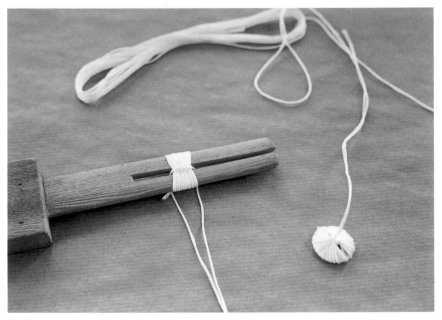

Tying the centre of the tuft

UNBORDERED EDGES

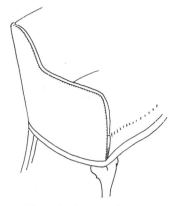

Typical unbordered edges
on a wing chair

Lightly upholstered, unbordered edges appear on small armchairs and wing chairs. The design has a slim, delicate appearance and is typical of some eighteenth-century upholstery, copied later in the Victorian period. Basically, the edges are formed by bringing the inside and outside covers together along the centre of wings, arms and chair backs.

This technique requires a foundation of stuffing and a long strip of some strong fabric, such as a repp, twill or good quality calico. Tie in a light, even stuffing of hair – cotton or wool felt is also suitable – along the frame edge. To obtain a well-rounded shape, remove and radius the two timber edges before beginning the upholstery.

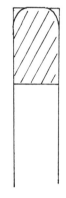

Radius the timber
edges before
beginning the
upholstery

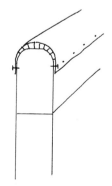

Tension and tack the cloth
strip lengthways

Cover the first stuffing with the cloth strip and tension it lengthways to achieve a good smooth surface, then tack it down each side of the frame edge. If the frame is curved, you may have to snip the cloth to allow it to sit well. Excess cloth will need to be trimmed away on any sharp bends or corners.

When the foundation is in place, continue the upholstery on the insides, followed by the outsides, in the normal way. Position and fix the inside cover, then tension and pin the edges to the centre of the foundation cloth. If necessary, draw in a centre pencil line as a guide for pinning. The first edge can then be slip stitched along the line. Apply and fix the outside covers in the same way, up to the line. In this type of upholstery, the outside areas of the frame are padded as much as the inside areas. To conceal the slip stitching line, sew a small upholstery cord into the join.

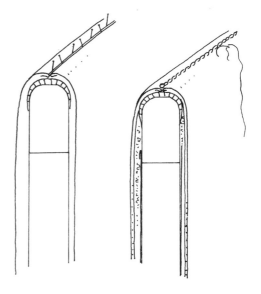

Tension and pin the inside and outside covers before slip stitching into place

Cover the stitching line with upholstery cord

The cording in place

UPHOLSTERED BRICKS

Well padded with cotton wadding and covered in a strong fabric, a house brick is a useful addition to the workshop. It can be used to hold down a piece of cover while it is being lightly stretched or laid out for cutting, and to hold patterns and templates steady while accurate marking out is being done.

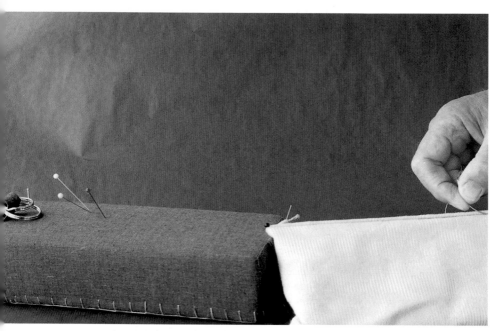

The weight keeps a fabric taut while you stitch

A covered brick will act as a third hand when you are setting two plies of fabric or stitching them together by hand. A border strip can be quickly pinned to the weight while a running stitch or an overedge stitch is being put in prior to gathering. Such a weight has dozens of uses in the preparation of materials for upholstery.

When the brick is being covered, sew in a couple of tabs, one at each end, so that pinning is convenient and easy. If preferred, a long pin can be inserted permanently into one end and then bent to form a sharp vertical hook.

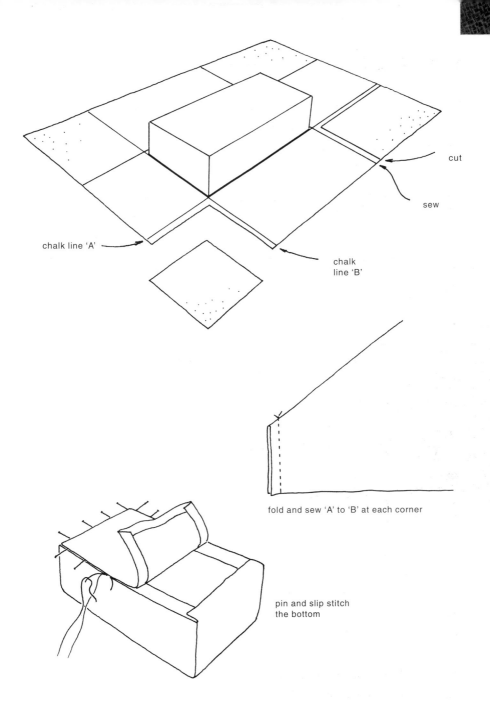

cut

sew

chalk line 'A'

chalk line 'B'

fold and sew 'A' to 'B' at each corner

pin and slip stitch the bottom

One method of covering a brick

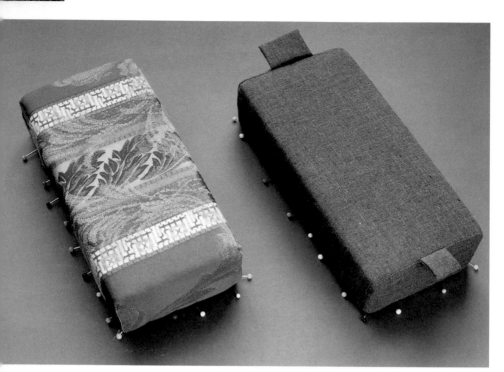

The upholstered brick

This provides an instant fixing. For example, a cushion cover can be hooked onto the weight while it is being closed and finished with a slip stitch. The brick will also act as a temporary pincushion while the work is being done.

Covered in an oddment of interesting upholstery fabric, or perhaps a purpose-made tapestry, a brick will make a very practical doorstop.

UPHOLSTERY NAILS

When you want to close nail with brass or antique upholstery nails, it is useful to know roughly how many nails will be needed. Estimating an amount before you begin is simple if you allow three nails of the standard 1660 size to 25mm (1in) of seating. Three nails with a 1mm (¹⁄₁₆in) space between them measures a little over 25mm (1in). Working on the basis that it is better to have more than you need, measure the lengths to be nailed and multiply this to allow at least three to the inch. There is always some waste in nailing, because nails do occasionally bend and sometimes a head will fly off.

Large and decorative upholstery nails

Buying small amounts and buying loose is expensive. Upholstery nails are packed in boxes of 1,000 and this is by far the best way of buying them. Buy a whole box or share the cost with a friend.

For spaced nailing, where the nails are put in at 1 or 1¼in (25 or 30mm) centres, it is easy to estimate the numbers required.

25mm (1in)

gimp pins

close nailing

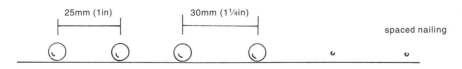

25mm (1in)   30mm (1¼in)

spaced nailing

Positioning nails

Good quality fancy nails, French nails and the large nails with brass heads are all very expensive. In this case, buying only those that you need is sensible, so estimating numbers is important.

Large brass upholstery nails spaced on an unsplit hide

Enamelled studs used to fix an outside chair back

VANDYKING

The technique used to join two fabrics when deep buttoning, so that the join is hidden beneath the pleating, is called vandyking. The fabrics can be laid and overlapped by hand or sewn before buttoning begins, either by hand or by machine.

The name given to zigzag joins in fabric comes from a fashion in dress made famous by the Flemish painter, Sir Anthony Van Dyck, in the mid-seventeenth century. The style of dress common in his paintings had collars, cloaks, and lace edges bordered to a series of large points. The name, in this context, has since become anglicized to 'vandyke'.

Working the join in by hand does allow for some variation in the positioning of buttons and the amount of overlap. Some flexibility is often needed when working on shaped work, such as chair backs, and when buttoning over edges. The ability to adjust the amounts of fabric being folded in and overlapped is one advantage of working the join by hand. However, if the buttoning can be planned in advance and marked out accurately on the reverse side of the cover, then sewing is a good solution. This will mean that the buttoning can go ahead quite rapidly and the join will be absorbed into the buttoning.

By hand

When a single row of buttons is being worked, the join will be a simple overlap with even pleating running through each button position.

If two rows of buttons are required, this creates a half-diamond. The folds between buttons will alternate so that they all face down to the base of the work. The join will still be simple, in the form of a good overlap. At the lower button point, you will need to make a cut so that the fabric can be turned in and pleated over the adjoining piece.

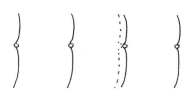

a single row of buttons

Three or more rows of buttons will create full diamonds. This again means that at each button point along the join, both pieces of cover will have to be cut or snipped to allow alternative folding in. All the pleats can then be laid face down. If a seat is being buttoned, lay the pleating to face forward.

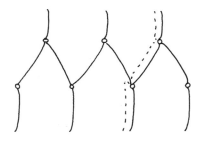

two rows make a half diamond

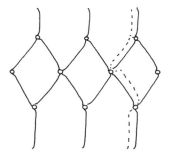

three rows form whole diamonds

Different shapes are created according to the number of rows of buttons

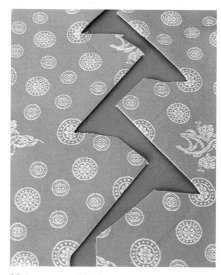

Make cuts and folds as you bring the two fabrics together

Assemble the join with the folds facing down the work

By machine

To produce a sewn vandyke join, mark out the reverse side of the two pieces to be joined with the buttoning pattern, then cut each, with a sewing allowance of 10mm (⅜in), in a zigzag formation running down the cloth. To allow for the sharp turns as the two pieces are sewn together, make a snip with the scissors at each button point to allow a flat seam to be sewn. The fabrics are then ready for buttoning in as required.

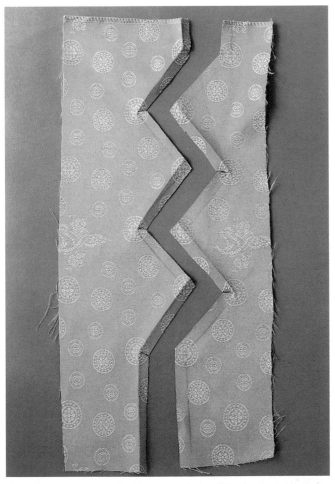

A vandyke join prepared and cut with 10mm (⅜in) sewing allowance

The reverse side of the join, after sewing the two edges together

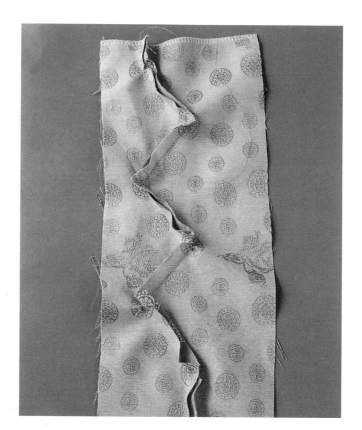

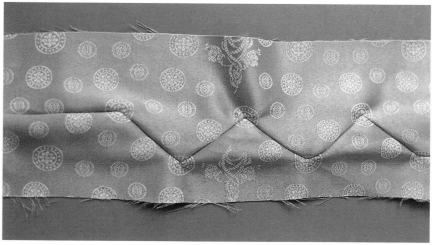

The completed join, ready for buttoning

WAXING

Applying a fine coat of beeswax to a twine or thread will help you to produce tight, well-formed stitchwork. A large block of beeswax has several uses in the workshop. Cabinetmakers use it on saws, screws and blades to make working on difficult materials smoother and to ease drawer runners and sliding timber parts.

For upholstery purposes, the wax block is set on the edge of the bench and a length of twine is drawn down through the edge of the wax to coat it. As it is drawn through the wax, some of the twist will be taken out. This produces twine which works well and is less likely to knot or twist, making hand stitchwork easier. Waxed twine will also have more grip on the materials through which it passes and so makes stitching more positive. Slip stitching, blind stitching and mattress stitching are all assisted by waxing.

Waxing also makes a length of twine a little stronger, thus extending its life. Cords, twines and threads can be treated in this way.

Waxing twine will strengthen it and take out some of the twist, making it easier to handle when stitching

WELL SEAT

Soft, deep areas of stuffing are created in seats and backs by making a well surrounded by a roll edge. This method is used as an alternative to a first and second stuffing in scrim, which is generally a very firm type of upholstery.

A close running stitch holds the scrim in place, to form the well

Chair backs, whether sprung or unsprung, need to feel soft and comfortable and to gradually shape themselves to the sitting human form. The inside back on a Victorian button-back chair is typical of the well construction with its a surrounding stitched edge and a firm lumbar area at the base.

Music stools of various designs, often adjustable, are another example where the well seat method provides the right type of upholstery for the sitter.

A well can be built onto a solid timber base, a webbed base or a sprung base. The edge is formed and stitched, and the centre then filled in to a good depth, depending on the feel and density required. The well seat is also put

scrim tacked into the
well on a wood base

scrim stitched down
on a webbed base

the scrim stitched onto
the spring hessian

a well with a thin first
stuffing of hair or fibre
in the centre

Various examples of well seat construction

to good use for platform seats in chairs when a cushion is to be supported
and held in place. The crown of the cushion sits comfortably into the well
when the second stuffing is kept low for this purpose.

WORKSPACE

An awful lot of time can be wasted searching for tools, bits, and pieces when they are needed, particularly with those items we use all the time. A well-organized workspace makes a huge difference and keeps frustration levels low. One or two wall shelves immediately behind your workbench can house most frequently used pieces. Essential items that should be quickly and easily accessible are tacks. Make a partitioned box to hold four or five different size tacks. This can be mobile or fixed on a low shelf, near your workbench. Alternatively, fix a wooden batten to the wall behind your bench from which to hang tack bags made from vinyl fabric, one for each different size. The bags can be tapped with a hammer to loosen them when they are needed. A needle pad kept in a fixed position is an excellent way to safely house needles and regulators, etc. Use a separate pad for the smaller items such as skewers, pins, and smaller circular needles. Twines, cords and threads can also be housed together, kept in plastic tubs on a shelf, with skeins of slipping thread hanging from a nail or two.

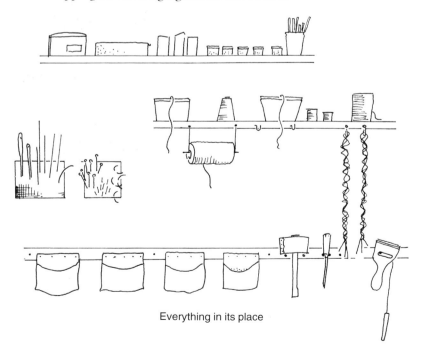

Everything in its place

ABOUT THE AUTHOR

The beech tree produces one of the best-known hardwoods used in the construction of upholstered chair frames, and this tree grows in profusion in the Chiltern Hills around High Wycombe, where David James was born. David has spent most of his working life in the furniture industry, including the areas of higher and further education, and consultancy.

Today he is a member of the lecturing team on the BA (Hons) Furniture Restoration and Craftsmanship course at the Buckinghamshire Chilterns University College in High Wycombe. His recent work as an upholstery consultant includes unusual wall coverings, tented ceilings and projects involving the conservation of historic upholstery.

He has written four previous books, all published by GMC Publications: *Upholstery: A Complete Course* (1990, revised 1999); *Upholstery Techniques and Projects* (1994); *The Upholsterer's Pocket Reference Book* (1996); and *Upholstery Restoration* (1997). He has also made two videos with GMC Publications under the general title *The Traditional Upholstery Workshop:* Part I, *Drop-in and Pinstuffed Seats*, and Part II, *Stuffover Upholstery* (both 1994).

WOODCARVING

The Art of the Woodcarver	GMC Publications
Carving Architectural Detail in Wood:	
The Classical Tradition	Frederick Wilbur
Carving Birds & Beasts	GMC Publications
Carving Nature: Wildlife Studies in Wood	Frank Fox-Wilson
Carving on Turning	Chris Pye
Carving Realistic Birds	David Tippey
Decorative Woodcarving	Jeremy Williams
Elements of Woodcarving	Chris Pye
Essential Tips for Woodcarvers	GMC Publications
Essential Woodcarving Techniques	Dick Onians
Further Useful Tips for Woodcarvers	GMC Publications
Lettercarving in Wood: A Practical Course	Chris Pye
Making & Using Working Drawings for	
Realistic Model Animals	Basil Fordham
Power Tools for Woodcarving	David Tippey
Practical Tips for Turners & Carvers	GMC Publications
Relief Carving in Wood: A Practical Introduction	Chris Pye
Understanding Woodcarving	GMC Publications
Understanding Woodcarving in the Round	GMC Publications
Useful Techniques for Woodcarvers	GMC Publications
Wildfowl Carving – Volume 1	Jim Pearce
Wildfowl Carving – Volume 2	Jim Pearce
The Woodcarvers	GMC Publications
Woodcarving: A Complete Course	Ron Butterfield
Woodcarving: A Foundation Course	Zoë Gertner
Woodcarving for Beginners	GMC Publications
Woodcarving Tools & Equipment	
Test Reports	GMC Publications
Woodcarving Tools, Materials & Equipment	Chris Pye

WOODTURNING

Adventures in Woodturning	David Springett
Bert Marsh: Woodturner	Bert Marsh
Bill Jones' Notes from the Turning Shop	Bill Jones
Bill Jones' Further Notes from the Turning Shop	Bill Jones
Bowl Turning Techniques Masterclass	Tony Boase
Colouring Techniques for Woodturners	Jan Sanders
The Craftsman Woodturner	Peter Child
Decorative Techniques for Woodturners	Hilary Bowen
Faceplate Turning	GMC Publications
Fun at the Lathe	R.C. Bell
Further Useful Tips for Woodturners	GMC Publications
Illustrated Woodturning Techniques	John Hunnex
Intermediate Woodturning Projects	GMC Publications
Keith Rowley's Woodturning Projects	Keith Rowley
Multi-Centre Woodturning	Ray Hopper
Practical Tips for Turners & Carvers	GMC Publications
Spindle Turning	GMC Publications
Turning Green Wood	Michael O'Donnell
Turning Miniatures in Wood	John Sainsbury

Turning Pens and Pencils	Kip Christensen & Rex Burningham
Turning Wooden Toys	Terry Lawrence
Understanding Woodturning	Ann & Bob Phillips
Useful Techniques for Woodturners	GMC Publications
Useful Woodturning Projects	GMC Publications
Woodturning: Bowls, Platters, Hollow Forms, Vases,	
Vessels, Bottles, Flasks, Tankards, Plates	GMC Publications
Woodturning: A Foundation	
Course (New Edition)	Keith Rowley
Woodturning: A Fresh Approach	Robert Chapman
Woodturning: An Individual Approach	Dave Regester
Woodturning: A Source Book of Shapes	John Hunnex
Woodturning Jewellery	Hilary Bowen
Woodturning Masterclass	Tony Boase
Woodturning Techniques	GMC Publications
Woodturning Tools & Equipment	
Test Reports	GMC Publications
Woodturning Wizardry	David Springett

WOODWORKING

Bird Boxes and Feeders for the Garden	Dave Mackenzie
Complete Woodfinishing	Ian Hosker
David Charlesworth's Furniture-Making	
Techniques	David Charlesworth
Furniture & Cabinetmaking Projects	GMC Publications
Furniture-Making Projects for the	
Wood Craftsman	GMC Publications
Furniture-Making Techniques for the	
Wood Craftsman	GMC Publications
Furniture Projects	Rod Wales
Furniture Restoration (Practical Crafts)	Kevin Jan Bonner
Furniture Restoration and Repair	
for Beginners	Kevin Jan Bonner
Furniture Restoration Workshop	Kevin Jan Bonner
Green Woodwork	Mike Abbott
Making & Modifying Woodworking Tools	Jim Kingshott
Making Chairs and Tables	GMC Publications
Making Classic English Furniture	Paul Richardson
Making Fine Furniture	Tom Darby
Making Little Boxes from Wood	John Bennett
Making Shaker Furniture	Barry Jackson
Making Woodwork Aids and Devices	Robert Wearing
Minidrill: Fifteen Projects	John Everett
Pine Furniture Projects for the Home	Dave Mackenzie
Router Magic: Jigs, Fixtures and Tricks to	
Unleash your Router's Full Potential	Bill Hylton
Routing for Beginners	Anthony Bailey
Scrollsaw Pattern Book	John Everett
The Scrollsaw: Twenty Projects	John Everett
Sharpening: The Complete Guide	Jim Kingshott
Sharpening Pocket Reference Book	Jim Kingshott
Space-Saving Furniture Projects	Dave Mackenzie
Stickmaking: A Complete Course	Andrew Jones & Clive George
Stickmaking Handbook	Andrew Jones & Clive George

Test Reports: *The Router* and	
Furniture & Cabinetmaking	*GMC Publications*
Veneering: A Complete Course	*Ian Hosker*
Woodfinishing Handbook (Practical Crafts)	*Ian Hosker*
Woodworking with the Router:	
Professional Router Techniques any	*Bill Hylton &*
Woodworker can Use	*Fred Matlack*
The Workshop	*Jim Kingshott*

UPHOLSTERY

Seat Weaving (Practical Crafts)	*Ricky Holdstock*
The Upholsterer's Pocket Reference Book	*David James*
Upholstery: A Complete Course	
(Revised Edition)	*David James*
Upholstery Restoration	*David James*
Upholstery Techniques & Projects	*David James*
Upholstery Tips and Hints	*David James*

DOLLS' HOUSES & MINIATURES

Architecture for Dolls' Houses	*Joyce Percival*
A Beginners' Guide to the Dolls' House Hobby	*Jean Nisbett*
The Complete Dolls' House Book	*Jean Nisbett*
The Dolls' House 1/24 Scale:	
A Complete Introduction	*Jean Nisbett*
Dolls' House Accessories, Fixtures and Fittings	*Andrea Barham*
Dolls' House Bathrooms: Lots of Little Loos	*Patricia King*
Dolls' House Fireplaces and Stoves	*Patricia King*
Easy to Make Dolls' House Accessories	*Andrea Barham*
Heraldic Miniature Knights	*Peter Greenhill*
Make Your Own Dolls' House Furniture	*Maurice Harper*
Making Dolls' House Furniture	*Patricia King*
Making Georgian Dolls' Houses	*Derek Rowbottom*
Making Miniature Gardens	*Freida Gray*
Making Miniature Oriental	
Rugs & Carpets	*Meik & Ian McNaughton*
Making Period Dolls' House Accessories	*Andrea Barham*
Making 1/12 Scale Character Figures	*James Carrington*
Making Tudor Dolls' Houses	*Derek Rowbottom*
Making Victorian Dolls' House Furniture	*Patricia King*
Miniature Bobbin Lace	*Roz Snowden*
Miniature Embroidery for the	
Georgian Dolls' House	*Pamela Warner*
Miniature Embroidery for the	
Victorian Dolls' House	*Pamela Warner*
Miniature Needlepoint Carpets	*Janet Granger*
More Miniature Oriental	
Rugs & Carpets	*Meik & Ian McNaughton*
The Secrets of the Dolls' House Makers	*Jean Nisbett*

VIDEOS

Drop-in and Pinstuffed Seats	*David James*
Stuffover Upholstery	*David James*
Elliptical Turning	*David Springett*
Woodturning Wizardry	*David Springett*
Turning Between Centres: The Basics	*Dennis White*
Turning Bowls	*Dennis White*
Boxes, Goblets and Screw Threads	*Dennis White*
Novelties and Projects	*Dennis White*
Classic Profiles	*Dennis White*
Twists and Advanced Turning	*Dennis White*
Sharpening the Professional Way	*Jim Kingshott*
Sharpening Turning & Carving Tools	*Jim Kingshott*
Bowl Turning	*John Jordan*
Hollow Turning	*John Jordan*
Woodturning: A Foundation Course	*Keith Rowley*
Carving a Figure: The Female Form	*Ray Gonzalez*
The Router: A Beginner's Guide	*Alan Goodsell*
The Scroll Saw: A Beginner's Guide	*John Burke*

MAGAZINES

WOODTURNING ◆ WOODCARVING

FURNITURE & CABINETMAKING

THE DOLLS' HOUSE MAGAZINE

THE ROUTER ◆ BUSINESSMATTERS

WATER GARDENING

EXOTIC GARDENING

OUTDOOR PHOTOGRAPHY

WOODWORKING

The above represents a selection of titles currently
published or scheduled to be published.
All are available direct from the Publishers or through
bookshops, newsagents and specialist retailers.
To place an order, or to obtain a complete catalogue, contact:

**GMC Publications,
Castle Place, 166 High Street,
Lewes, East Sussex BN7 1XU,
United Kingdom
Tel: 01273 488005 Fax: 01273 478606
E-mail: pubs@thegmcgroup.com**

Orders by credit card are accepted